T0315040

Incident Management for Operations

Rob Schnepp, Ron Vidal, and Chris Hawley

Beijing · Boston · Farnham · Sebastopol · Tokyo

Incident Management for Operations

by Rob Schnepp, Ron Vidal, and Chris Hawley

Published by O'Reilly Media, Inc., 1005 Gravenstein Highway North, Sebastopol, CA 95472.

O'Reilly books may be purchased for educational, business, or sales promotional use. Online editions are also available for most titles (*http://oreilly.com/safari*). For more information, contact our corporate/institutional sales department: 800-998-9938 or *corporate@oreilly.com*.

Editor: Brian Anderson	**Indexer:** WordCo Indexing Services, Inc.
Production Editor: Shiny Kalapurakkel	**Interior Designer:** Monica Kamsvaag
Copyeditor: Gillian McGarvey	**Cover Designer:** Karen Montgomery
Proofreader: Kim Cofer	**Illustrator:** Rebecca Demarest

July 2017:   First Edition

Revision History for the First Edition

2017-06-20:   First Release

See *http://www.oreilly.com/catalog/errata.csp?isbn=0636920036159* for release details.

978-1-491-91762-6

[LSI]

Contents

Foreword

This book originated from an argument during my first year as Amazon's "Master of Disaster," as I began applying the incident management and operations practices I learned as a firefighter to improve Amazon's overall reliability and resiliency. I vividly remember facing a room full of scowling engineers and managers who were saying, "I get that these ideas work for firefighters, but do you really think they can work at internet speed?"

The answer, of course, was yes. The systems and best practices developed over decades of managing complex emergency incidents—where seconds count and lives are on the line—work just as well for managing complex incidents for technology organizations. Over the next few years, my team and I used these techniques and systems to help transform the culture and technology of what is now one of the greatest engineering and operations organizations in the world.

When I left Amazon, it was clear to me that as the world was becoming increasingly connected and distributed, people would come to depend on the new technology we build and systems we run as part of their daily lives. It was also clear to me and a group of passionate peers that there were too few people with the knowledge and experience to build and run these systems at scale. My friend, Artur Bergman helped me found the O'Reilly Velocity Performance & Operations conference to organize, develop, and spread our emerging and critical professional discipline.

As Velocity grew, I started sharing my work with friends and mentors in the Fire Service. I am fortunate to have worked with and been trained by some of the most experienced and respected incident management experts in the world, and I asked them to help build and expand on what I had started.

I convened the first "Web Ops/Fire Ops" summit on a beautiful day at Artur's loft in San Francisco. Attending from "the internet" were Artur Bergman (Fastly/Wikia), John Adams (Twitter), Johnathan Heiliger (Facebook), Pedro

Canahuati (Facebook), Simon Wistow (Fastly), and Chris Brown (Amazon/Chef/Microsoft). Attending from the "Fire Ops" side were the authors of this book: Chris Hawley, Rob Schnepp, and Ron Vidal.

After a few hours of sharing backgrounds, "war stories," and a lot of laughter, it became clear to everyone that there was both the need and opportunity for a tech-oriented incident management training program. Chris, Rob, and Ron formed Blackrock Partners and began consulting with large companies on how to improve their operations. Since then they have worked with dozens of tech companies, trained thousands of new responders, and reviewed hundreds of incidents as they help companies "work like a fire department at internet speed."

This book is the first publicly released product of their exceptional work, and is the essential foundation for building technology and organizations that people can depend on. I hope you use it.

As we say in the fire department, "See you at the big one!"

—Jesse Robbins
Founder and CEO,
Orion Labs, Inc.

Preface

Does your company have IT incidents?

Have you ever had a high-severity IT incident that disrupted the service your customers rely on you to provide?

Did that incident damage your company's reputation, erode trust with your customers or investors, or create adverse business or financial impact?

Was the incident response and resolution slow, unorganized, or poorly managed?

If you answered "Yes" to any of these questions, ask yourself one more question: are you happy with how your company currently responds to IT incidents? If the answer is "No," then you must be looking for a better way, and this book was written for you.

We will show you a new way to think about responding to and resolving IT incidents. This new way works in small DevOps teams all the way up to the largest enterprise and service provider organizations. Collectively, we have more than 100 years of incident command experience leading special operations teams in busy urban fire departments on the east and west coasts and managing critical infrastructure throughout the United States. We also have specialized incident management experience in more than 40 countries at the highest levels of government and industry. In this book, we identify the best practices from outside the IT industry that have literally undergone trial by fire, and apply the same incident response methodology to the world of IT operations.

For more than 40 years, fire departments throughout the United States have used a framework to organize and lead the talent and resources required to respond to emergencies of all kinds. This framework is called the *Incident Management System* (IMS) and it's a simple and effective way to organize your team rapidly when bad things happen. IMS was designed as an all-hazard, all-risk incident management framework.

How and why did we make the jump from the fire service to IT? In the fall of 2012, at the suggestion of Jesse Robbins (see Foreword), the original adopter of using IMS tactics and strategies in IT, we met with a select group of IT professionals who were responsible for uptime at large social media companies and other large-scale web operations. The goal of the meeting was to discuss and better understand the challenges faced by IT companies when it comes to resolving IT incidents. These IT professionals wanted to look outside their industry for a better way because the models inside the IT industry were not working well. They wanted to hear how the fire service manages time-sensitive incidents in which the stakes are high, the decision-making environment is poor, the conditions are changing, and the outcomes are uncertain.

As the discussion progressed, the group recognized the striking similarities between urgent public safety incidents requiring a fire department response and urgent technology incidents requiring an IT response. In fact, the first IT people to respond to a service disruption or a cybersecurity attack are the "first responders," just like the first firefighters on the scene of a fire. By the end of the meeting, we all agreed that there were significant opportunities to translate the best parts of the public safety IMS, especially as it pertains to leading people and managing time, directly to the IT industry. The principles are the same and directly applicable to the type of high severity/priority incidents experienced by the IT industry.

"A few years ago, we looked for a better way to manage incidents at Salesforce," says Kwesi Ames, VP of Site Reliability Engineering at the company. "By adapting the principles of IMS, the same system used by firefighters, we saw a tremendous improvement in responding to critical technology incidents. It was a real game changer for us," he emphasized. "It provided a disciplined template that allowed us to be consistently efficient in our response and handling of major issues in our production environment. This has resulted in faster recovery times and minimized loss of customer trust."

IMS establishes the framework of incident response and the norms of behavior for the incident responders. High severity/priority events place the incident responders under critical time pressure to resolve IT incidents when customer trust, adverse financial impacts, and the company's reputation are at stake. Using IMS increases your chances at having a good outcome and protecting the company's business.

It is a fact that the future of computing promises more scale, more complexity, and certainly more change—all at greater and greater speed. It's also true that the odds increase every day that your organization will have a major technology incident, created internally or externally.

Without a predictable way to respond to incidents, any organization—growing or mature—is at risk. Torsten Rueter, global platform services leader at GE Capital, looks at it this way: "Frameworks such as ITIL have helped mature large-scale IT operations. The Incident Management System addresses some of the more subtle—yet extremely important—aspects of managing incidents. Without strong leadership, collaboration, and shared working patterns, an Incident Response Team won't live up to its full potential."

Building on Jesse Robbin's work, we adapted the Incident Management System (IMS) from public safety to corporate IT environments. We incorporate IMS into ITIL, DevOps, Agile, and Lean practices. We collaborate with customers to build a culture of incident response.

We bring a unique viewpoint to the IT industry. Collectively, we bring over 100 years of fire service and critical infrastructure experience to IT incident management. We blend our deep global experience in fire, hazardous materials (HazMat), weapons of mass destruction (WMD), and counterterrorism incident response with fiber networks, data centers, oil and gas, power, and capital markets to improve incident management performance.

Our customers generate $400 billion of revenue and create $1 trillion of market cap, while employing over 850,000 people around the world. These companies rank in the top 10% of the Fortune 500 and PwC Global 100 Software Leaders, operating globally in the industrial, financial services, consumer products, telecommunications, and software sectors, serving markets in North America, Europe, the Middle East, Africa, Asia, and the Pacific.

Assessment, training, evaluation, and exercises are the best predictor of future performance. We've delivered our incident management programs across three continents and into nine countries to thousands of Incident Commanders (IC), subject matter experts (SME), executives, and corporate staff. They work on site reliability, cybersecurity, mission-critical support, unified command, enterprise IT, operations, R&D and engineering/technology (network, database, SAN/ Storage, server, automation, applications), legal, crisis communications, and executive management teams. Those teams work in global command centers, emergency operations centers, regional operations centers, war rooms, and board rooms at some of the biggest companies running the largest technology stacks in the world. We maximize uptime during high severity IT incidents.

This book will show you a best practice in incident management for the IT industry, even though it's from outside the IT industry. We'll offer not just a better way to think about incident response but a look inside the battle-tested techniques of IMS used in other IT organizations and throughout the United States fire service to organize, lead, and resolve life-or-death situations. We will offer the same thoughts, perspectives, and advice that helped a Fortune 50 financial services company reduce their Mean Time To Repair (MTTR) by 35%. Also, we'll discuss use cases representative of some of the largest (and some of the smallest) IT operations teams in the world.

There is a better way to respond to incidents, and you just found it.

Conventions Used in This Book

The following typographical conventions are used in this book:

Italic

> Indicates new terms, URLs, email addresses, filenames, and file extensions.

O'Reilly Safari

 *Safari* (formerly Safari Books Online) is a membership-based training and reference platform for enterprise, government, educators, and individuals.

Members have access to thousands of books, training videos, Learning Paths, interactive tutorials, and curated playlists from over 250 publishers, including O'Reilly Media, Harvard Business Review, Prentice Hall Professional, Addison-Wesley Professional, Microsoft Press, Sams, Que, Peachpit Press, Adobe, Focal

Press, Cisco Press, John Wiley & Sons, Syngress, Morgan Kaufmann, IBM Redbooks, Packt, Adobe Press, FT Press, Apress, Manning, New Riders, McGraw-Hill, Jones & Bartlett, and Course Technology, among others.

For more information, please visit *http://oreilly.com/safari.*

How to Contact Us

Please address comments and questions concerning this book to the publisher:

O'Reilly Media, Inc.
1005 Gravenstein Highway North
Sebastopol, CA 95472
800-998-9938 (in the United States or Canada)
707-829-0515 (international or local)
707-829-0104 (fax)

To comment or ask technical questions about this book, send email to *bookquestions@oreilly.com.*

For more information about our books, courses, conferences, and news, see our website at *http://www.oreilly.com.*

Find us on Facebook: *http://facebook.com/oreilly*

Follow us on Twitter: *http://twitter.com/oreillymedia*

Watch us on YouTube: *http://www.youtube.com/oreillymedia*

We have a web page for this book, where we list errata, examples, and any additional information. You can access this page at *http://shop.oreilly.com/product/0636920036159.do*

Acknowledgments

The authors would like to thank the staff at O'Reilly Media for all their support and assistance, especially Brian Anderson who guided us through the process. In addition, the authors would like to thank Jesse Robbins, who had the foresight and vision to bring the IMS concepts to the IT world. In addition to being a wonderful friend, he has provided a tremendous amount of advice and counsel to each of us, for which we are very grateful. Another person who was invaluable in the development of this text was Andrea Walter, who did our initial editing and formatting. She had a challenging task in wrangling our thoughts into this text. Tom Welch, a Fire Chief from the San Francisco Bay area weighed in on the text, providing insights and comments on the content from a fire service perspective. We would also like to thank our reviewers who provided the guidance on enhancing this text: Jason Hand and John Allspaw. Ashley and Amber Vidal provided edits and honest feedback, which helped streamline and explain our points in plain English as well. We must also acknowledge our customers and the thousands of IT responders we have trained and interacted with around the world. They are contributors to this as much as we are in that their experiences, challenges, and success are brought to you in the pages of this book.

Evaluating the Incident Response PROCESS

Definition of *incident*:

> *An occurrence, either human-caused or a natural phenomenon, that requires action or support by emergency services personnel to prevent or minimize loss of life or damage to property and/or natural resources. (National Fire Protection Association)*
>
> *An unplanned interruption to an IT service or reduction in the quality of an IT service. (ITIL)*

As you read this sentence, IT incidents are happening all over the world. The response to those incidents comes in many forms, from one person working on an issue to a large group of people dialing into a conference call bridge or typing into a plethora of communications/workflow/productivity applications from anywhere around the globe. Those responders may use ITIL process or DevOps principles or an internally created system or some other method. The response may be completely organized or totally chaotic. But, one way or another, IT incidents are being resolved. The real question is: "Are they being resolved *as quickly as they could be?*"

Note

For illustration throughout the book, we will use a conference call bridge as the example of IRT communications. There are many methods used to communicate during an incident, including verbal and written communications across many technology platforms, and not all IRTs use conference bridges for incident response, but depicting the spoken word serves as an effective platform to illustrate interpersonal communications.

The first step in the journey toward efficient and well-organized incident response begins with an honest evaluation of the status quo, including the Incident Lifecycle (see Figure 1-1). In many cases, incident responders find their way into a pattern of responding (either good or bad) and end up sticking with it out of inertia. Some responders may have survived a significant incident and say "wow, that was a close call, hope that never happens again." Patterns and habits, by their very nature, are comfortable to maintain and difficult to break.

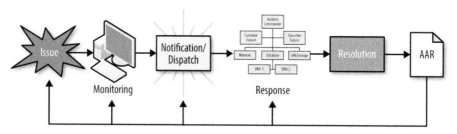

Figure 1-1. The Incident Lifecycle

Regardless of whether you are happy or unhappy with the way your Incident Response Team (IRT) responds to IT emergencies, it is wise to investigate if performance can be improved.

Note

For the sake of consistency, the remainder of this book will use the term Incident Response Team (IRT) as a general term for the group tasked with mitigating incidents within an organization. Your particular group may have a different term or organizational structure for responding to incidents.

After all, incidents pose risk to the company in many ways, none of them good: tarnished reputation; erosion of customer trust; diminished brand; adverse financial impacts and loss of investor confidence. Successful and efficient Incident Response Teams share common characteristics, all of which are easy to identify once you know what to look for. Separate and apart from an After Action Review (AAR) (see Chapter 6), which takes place after the response, it may be useful for you to evaluate your entire incident response process as it exists today and see if there are areas that could be improved.

To begin, it is useful to develop a list of general questions that can be asked and answered both quantitatively and qualitatively. Having good baseline data on past response statistics and/or how your response team is set up helps lay the foundation for evaluation.

If you are a small organization with just a few people, it might seem obvious who will respond to resolve incidents. One of the first questions we ask organizations is this: *Is there one person here who understands the entire stack in great detail to fix any issue that may occur?* The obvious answer is *no*, but we have validated this with organizations around the world. Plus, as businesses grow and scale, the entire stack will continue to get more complicated, requiring more specialized problem solvers, which will require a more mature incident management process. If your organization acquires companies to expand its business and portfolio of products and services, incident management processes at the acquired companies should also be identified, evaluated, and reviewed during the due diligence phase of the deal. Irrespective of how your organization grows, ask yourself questions like the following to narrow your focus on how to best configure the Incident Response Team.

This list of questions is certainly not exhaustive and is meant to simply stimulate your own thinking about how to lay a foundation for an Incident Response Team evaluation:

- What is your definition of an *incident* and *event*?
- How many incidents do you respond to in a given month?
- What is the ratio of incidents to events and do you respond the same way to both?
- How many incidents occurred per month over the last two years?
- How many events occurred per month over the last two years?
- Identify and describe current severity/priority levels for incident response.
- Are incident severity/priority levels used and/or consistently applied throughout the incident response organization?

- What reports/data analysis regarding incident response do you have?
- In your opinion, are incidents managed and directed in a consistent and efficient manner? If not, list the challenges/obstacles.
- When an incident occurs, is there a defined plan for response and escalation?
- Is there a core team with 24x7 on-duty responsibilities or is the team on call?
- List all potential incident responders (Incident Commanders and SMEs) by business unit and geographic location.
- Describe shift schedule and staffing levels for the primary Incident Response Team, by location and function.
- List third-party vendors that are part of the incident response by function, location, and contact information.
- Do IRT members have time standards for incident response? Are those time standards followed by responders and enforced by executive leadership?
- What challenges exist in terms of integrating SMEs into a response?
- Is there an organization chart for incident response that lists the primary Incident Response Team and all other participants?
- How do communications occur during an incident (e.g., conference call, web-based tools, etc.)?
- Are incident voice communications (e.g., conference bridges, WebEx, etc.) recorded? Archived? Reviewed?
- Is someone assigned to prepare and conduct the Root Cause Analysis (RCA) and AARs?
- Is there a process for incorporating information learned from AAR recommendations back into peacetime development/engineering?
- What role do senior executives play during an incident response?

Keep in mind that efficient incident response is all about process, with ten general but distinct steps in the Incident Lifecycle:

1. Detect the issue.

2. Determine if issue is an incident or an event.

3. Dispatch the appropriate Incident Response Team.

4. Assemble the response team mean time to assemble (MTTA).

5. Establish command, organize resources, and set incident objectives.

6. Lead the resolution effort using IMS.

7. Notify the appropriate stakeholders.

8. Resolve the incident and release resources.

9. Conduct AARs.

10. Implement quality improvement (QI) and quality assurance (QA) (covered in more detail later in the chapter).

Event: A point-in-time fact relevant to the operations of your infrastructure or application (e.g., CPU crossed the 95% threshold on host-abc or Change #1234 successfully deployed to host-abc) but which is not considered to be an incident. Events don't require the implementation of the Incident Management System (IMS) or an Incident Commander (IC). Events may turn into incidents.

You might come across a version of this list in a different order or perhaps with a different step here or there, but, for the most part, this is how an IT incident evolves. Figure 1-1 depicts the Incident Lifecycle. QA and QI are part of the AAR process, and not called out as separate items here.

We commonly run into Incident Response Teams that have been overwhelmed by an incident that got bigger and/or nastier and/or moved faster than they were prepared for. Perhaps they could not assemble the right technical resources quickly or were frustrated by the fact that only a few members of the team were "capable of running an incident." Or there may have been a lack of clear and directed leadership, resulting in chaos on the incident conference call bridge or some other communication channel. Successfully operating high-reliability, production environments depends on strong leadership and a capable team of technical experts in network, compute, storage, and applications, whether for a small DevOps team or a global enterprise team. In daily workflows, for example, DevOps is a team sport with a collaborative methodology that marches to a certain cadence. Incident response is also a team sport that depends on strong leadership and a capable team of technical experts, but the pace at which the team assembles and begins resolution is different than completing a sprint or some other nonincident-related task.

We've developed an acronym that represents the seven key attributes of an effective incident response program. PROCESS stands for *Predictable*, *Repeatable*, *Optimized*, *Clear*, *Evaluated*, *Scalable*, and *Sustainable*.

To that end, each letter of PROCESS is an interdependent link in the incident response chain. Use those links as a step-by-step analysis tool to evaluate how your current IT response approach measures up. The Incident Lifecycle is also a series of interrelated steps that builds progressively on the previous step and has influence on all the other downstream steps. As an example, if reducing your overall mean time to repair (MTTR) of an IT incident is important to the company, you must look at every element of the Incident Lifecycle, from detecting the presence of an issue, to how the team is dispatched and how long it takes to assemble the right team of people, all the way through the resolution effort and AAR.

Many companies waste valuable time early in the Incident Lifecycle due to inefficient dispatch of the responders. Additionally, we find many companies do not draw a clear distinction between a notification and a dispatch. It is typical to find no clear distinction between those who are "in the loop" of information regarding an incident and those who are called to respond.

Dispatch: The action of reaching out to a particular person representing a job function (database, network, storage, security, for example), team, or other group for the purpose of summoning a needed function to the incident. Dispatch is different than notification in that it is an order rather than a request. In the fire service, being dispatched is a directive to be followed like any other directive and is not a negotiation or considered to be optional.

Notification: A message (urgent or otherwise) sent to a person (e.g., SMS, phone, email), usually related to an alert or incident. Notifications are intended to be an FYI rather than a dispatch. Notifications are not a call to respond, although they may be used to inform people of events.

For purpose of comparison and clarity, think of it this way: people are notified and incident response functions are dispatched.

Alert: Represents the state of a monitoring tool check/condition initiated/resolved by an event (e.g., from Pingdom—your website is currently DOWN). Alerts are generated by tools monitoring technology for identifying an abnormality in the environment. Alerts may be the first point in time that an event is identified. Further investigation may determine whether the issue is an event or incident.

Some companies use the "spray and pray" or "group think" approach of sending out notifications to a bunch of technical experts, executives, and others, having dozens of them arrive on an open conference call bridge (or other communications method) with no identified leader, with the hope the group will resolve the issue in a reasonable amount of time. In practice, these groups meander their way to resolution. In other cases, there is no clear expectation that once alerted, an incident responder must arrive on a conference call bridge with any sense of urgency. Many companies are quite lax when it comes to defining and communicating clear expectations about being "on-call." If you are on-call, you are in the "right now" business, not the "I'll get around to it in a few minutes" business, or "I'm busy doing other things" business. Time is money and the longer it takes to dispatch and assemble the right team, the longer it takes to resolve the issue. You can get more responders or write more code, but you can't make any more time. Time can only be saved or wasted.

Tip

If you are an IT incident responder, *TIME* is the most important commodity that exists.

Many teams (and company executives) focus on asking about a Root Cause Analysis (RCA) of an issue in the first few minutes of an incident. This is the wrong question to ask. Asking "why it broke" (root cause) is far less important than "how do we fix it" (incident resolution). In our opinion, the first thing to focus on is the mean time to assemble (MTTA) the right team. You won't have good MTTRs with slow MTTAs! In the early stages of an incident, facts are being discovered as the situation unfolds. The best fact discoverers are the right technical subject matter experts (SMEs) responding to the incident, because they can look at logs, perform queries, and run analytics. These SMEs become the eyes and ears of the Incident Response Team. Without urgent MTTA from SMEs, there is no data. Without data, the Incident Response Team is flying blind and corrective action can't be taken. Focus on fixing the issue first and restoring service! As we say in the fire department, "when you put out the fire, conditions get better."

To that end, be hard on yourself and your expectations, and be realistic when it comes to evaluating your current incident response process. There are easy pick-ups in MTTA in most companies if the company is willing to set clear expectations. Think about this: the MTTA part of the Incident Lifecycle contains all of the activities prior to response. MTTA is the only activity that is controlled by the Incident Response Team! Incident resolution is a wild card as your operating environment is complex and conditions of the incident can change at any moment. We'll say it again for emphasis, MTTA is the only activity that is controlled by the Incident Response Team!

The answers that you find by using PROCESS as an evaluation template will differ from company to company, because a cookbook approach doesn't exist. This is more of a thought exercise you can use to explore and map the various aspects of a PROCESS-driven Incident Response Team, and to discover and correct any weaknesses in your system along the way.

PREDICTABLE

The foundation of excellent Incident Response Teams is *predictability*. Customers buy and expect 7x24x365 availability from their service providers. We know that 100% availability is a near impossible metric, so companies aim for 99.99% or greater. In fact, enormous investments are made with each incremental 9 to the right of the availability decimal point, improving from 99.99% to 99.999%. So, if ultimate availability is elusive in production environments, predictability in incident response is absolutely essential.

Predictability in incident response is about clarity of roles and responsibilities and the expected behavior of each person before and after they are assembled for an incident. It's about eliminating uncertainty in the assembly phase of the response.

Are there clear expectations for which SMEs might be required for a particular incident type, and who will take the leadership role of the Incident Commander? Efficient Incident Response Teams, no matter how big or small, have crisp, well defined on-call procedures and they hold people accountable!

Are your technical experts on-call in different time zones? Are there back-ups to the primary on-call personnel? Are they clear that "on-call" means ready to respond to a page, text, or other notification in a time frame specified by the company?

Having responders understand their role is critical to success. Incident response isn't about arriving to help resolve the issue when it's convenient. If you are identified as available on-call, it is not optional. Perhaps your regular day job keeps you crazy busy every day. If you are on-duty or on-call as an identified incident responder, make sure you are ready to respond quickly. Be ready, willing, and able to answer the call and protect the business!

Ensuring that response expectations are clear is the low-hanging fruit because it can be done in advance of the incident occurring. Identifying the players, or at least the type of players you might need, is a pre-planning exercise and can be largely scripted in a defined response plan and evaluated/refined as part of the AAR. Think about your last 10 incidents and evaluate the MTTA in terms of getting the right people to the response. Did you get the right people to respond quickly and with a sense of urgency? Did they perform and participate in a positive way? If not, why not? Think of predictability as the "who" part of the response.

REPEATABLE

If there is uncertainty about *who* will respond to an incident and *who* will be in charge, and *how* you bring them together for a response, then your incident response can be improved.

Repeatability is the "how" part of the response, with the goal of consistently and efficiently dispatching the people identified in the predictability section. Highly efficient Incident Response Teams have reviewed a list of common or likely incident types, assigned each a severity (SEV) level, identified SMEs by function to respond and matched the dispatch of SME responders to those severity levels. For example, a SEV level 1 may have a predetermined list of technical expertise (network, compute, storage, applications) that would be appropriate for a particular incident type. Each organization is different, so we aren't going to provide specific examples. Suffice it to say that timely identification of an IT incident, which drives a rapid and specific dispatch procedure with clear expectations about when and how the incident responders will convene (the quicker, the better) is the keystone to predictability. Repeatability demonstrates that every response to any type of incident should strive to be the same no matter what time of day, day of the week, or time of year it occurs. For example, predictable and repeatable responses should happen the same way at 2:00 A.M. on Christmas morning or 2:00 P.M. on any normal business day. Predictability and repeatability is the natural enemy of spray and pray!

This is not to say that an organization must have 24x7 operations to qualify for having a demonstrably repeatable response. It is more about the incident responders being truly available when they are designated to be on-call and responding in the same way every time.

OPTIMIZED

Optimization builds upon a predictable and repeatable incident response mechanism by ensuring the identified responders understand the rules of engagement during incidents and are trained, equipped, and clearly prepared to do what is being asked of them. Do you have a formal training program for responders (and we hope it's based on IMS!)? Is it provided consistently across your team, especially if the team is global? Does everyone understand how they fit into the incident response? Are there clear escalation policies in place? What conditions must be present to trigger an escalation? Who gets the escalation?

Escalation: The addition of more or different resources (SMEs, teams, outside vendors, etc.), beyond an initial dispatch, required to resolve an incident. As an example, the IC may need more or different database administrators (DBAs) on an incident, so the IC should escalate to those additional resources. Escalation can also mean to notify or otherwise contact internal stakeholders inside the company at a higher level than the IC. This could include escalating an incident to company executives.

If you interact with vendors or other third parties, do they know how to respond and participate? Do they share your same sense of urgency? Is the concept of incident command universally understood and implemented?

It's easy to spot those individuals that just "don't get it" in terms of having the sense of urgency and focus required to resolve an incident, or who feel inconvenienced by being on-call in the first place. However, was the importance of the incident response plan explained to them? Were they trained in their individual and team roles in incident response? Incident response is a team sport, and leaves no room for egos, attitude, or lack of trust within the team. It's important to hold people accountable but it's unfair if they are held accountable without ever being trained or briefed as to the company's expectations. In our consulting practice, we emphasize the need to identify all the potential Incident Commanders, technical SME experts, executives, vendors, and any others who may be called to respond. This allows us to ensure that they all have specific incident response training and a clear understating of the expectations, so that at minimum each incident responder knows what is expected of them and are prepared to contribute appropriately. Predictability is the *who* and repeatability is the *how* of incident response. Optimization is the part of PROCESS where you must ensure that everyone is trained and equipped to do the job!

CLEAR

Clarity ensures that general programmatic and incident response goals and objectives are conveyed to all IRT members and all others that may participate in a response. It's easy to assume that all who might join an incident response in any capacity are clear about the goals and objectives of the incident resolution effort. Unfortunately, this isn't always the case. Oftentimes, we find that IT responders aren't clear about why they are put on-call or asked to join an incident conference call bridge. We hear this frequently when we listen to recorded bridges for our clients. A technical expert will join and ask, "why am I here," or "why do you need me?" Some discussion occurs to get the expert oriented to the fact that they have been called in to help resolve an IT incident. Valuable time is wasted that can never be recovered. To that end, it is critical to ensure that anyone who might be called upon to respond knows exactly why they are being summoned, what their role will be, and when they will be released from the incident by the IC.

This expectation setting starts at the top of the company's organizational chart. It is mission critical that the executives set the tone for creating and supporting incident response by placing value on the effort, both within the IRT and across the company. Executives should strive to build a culture of incident response, ensuring predictability, repeatability, and optimization of the team. Again, it seems simple, but it's vital that all responders know and understand what's expected of them when they are called upon to respond, and that the incident consistency with which the team responds is ensured. For the incident response to be successful, this thought process and support must be baked into the company's culture. The nature of the IT incident can and will vary, but the incident response approach should be clear and consistent.

Do all responders really understand that they are, in essence, functioning as the fire department for the company? We hear many fire department related references from site reliability engineers, SMEs, and executives. As an example, the use of the word *triage* is commonly used in IT. Its origin is as a common emergency medical term, meaning to sort and assign priority during an incident with many victims. The first person who responds to an IT issue is literally a first responder. As the issue may grow into an incident, the response must also scale, much like a fire escalating to a second, third, or fourth alarm. What's strange is that many responders don't see the public-safety-responder-to-IT-responder connection, nor feel the sense of responsibility that goes along with it. "We are so busy putting out fires," said one engineer, "that I can't find time to do my day job!" Said another way, while the rest of the company is building the business, the incident responders should be defending the business from harm.

Think of the point of clarity in this way: we all don't need to think the same way during a response, but we must think in the same direction with the same viewpoint, unity of purpose, methodology, and focus.

EVALUATED

Up to this point, the emphasis has been on putting the pieces in place to create an excellent incident response program. We will discuss the AAR process in Chapter 6, but for now understand that each incident response creates an opportunity to learn how to better respond to the next one. As we've heard in incident management over the years, "don't let a good crisis go to waste!" Committing time and effort to objectively and specifically look at each part of the Incident Lifecycle, from the detection of an issue, dispatch of the incident responders and assembly of the Incident Response Team, through how the incident was ultimately resolved will most certainly offer lessons learned or areas that could be improved. The evaluation piece is where quality assurance (QA) and quality improvement (QI) efforts tie back to PROCESS.

Quality Assurance (QA)

Taking an objective look at a behavior, decision, or circumstance and evaluating it against the established standard, ensuring the expected behavior is occurring.

Quality Improvement (QI)
    Finding opportunities, weaknesses, or missing pieces of the incident
    response mechanism and taking steps to correct/improve the deficiency.

    QA and QI are investments that produce dividends over the long run. Tweak-
ing the incident response process, the way in which the technical experts
resolved the incident, and/or the leadership abilities of the Incident Commander
may uncover weaknesses that are hampering your pursuit of excellent performance. There is much work underway in the area of "blameless post mortems"
and we applaud those efforts. Today's IT environments are large and complex.
Not every use case can be anticipated or configuration tested for flawless operation with all of the other elements in the stack. Incidents also present the opportunity to find and correct defects. Let's create a learning culture where incident
information is used to improve the operations. It's all about getting better—not
finding fault or assigning blame!
    When you uncover "landmines" of poor or inconsistent performance, you
must identify them, acknowledge them, and do what it takes to improve the defi-
ciency. Absent any thoughtful way of objectively evaluating the incident response
process, poor performance may become the established norm and, culturally, it
will be more difficult to change down the road.

SCALABLE

A powerful characteristic of IMS is that it works both for the smallest startup
company with a few employees, to the largest companies with operations around
the world. The *scalable* part of process is linked to predictability and repeatability
in that a sound incident response process can quickly grow or shrink depending
on the needs of the incident or growth of the organization. The latter refers to
scalability at a program level rather than incident level, but as the organization
grows, so grows the need for a larger and deeper pool of resources. We refer to
this as *bench strength*. Bench strength is much like how sports teams look at scaling—having access to a wide variety of equally good talent to fill in the gaps for
rotating, resting, or replacing players for the duration of the game. For example,
as a company grows, the number of incidents will likely also grow and the company will need more qualified people to run production operations and incidents.
Bench strength contributes to both the scalable and sustainable nature of PRO-
CESS.
    For IT, it's important to acknowledge vacations, sick time, travel, shift cover-
age, etc. to maintain a high level of proficiency and availability of incident

responders at all times. Since it's unknown when the next big crippling incident might strike, the IT incident response process should be ever at the ready, just like a fire department. A team with good bench strength does not just have a handful of star players. It is comprised of a cadre of talent that can be interchanged, added, or expanded to meet whatever need is present. We have watched our customers' environments get larger and more complex, by combining the scaling of capacity planning for future demand with technology refresh programs, all in the velocity of continuous code releases. Consequently, these environments fail harder and will require more focused incident management efforts as time goes on.

Ideally, the Incident Response Team establishes its identity and available resources by function so that it is not dependent on only a handful of people to respond on a regular basis. Many IT environments are already so complex that it takes a constellation of specific technical expertise to understand all of the various operational details. It's quite common to require entire development teams, application teams, and database/storage/network experts to solve a single IT incident. With scale and complexity come even more specialization and the need to handle a larger volume and complexity of IT incidents, possibly happening concurrently. Therefore, being able to rapidly dispatch and obtain a greater number of varied and highly qualified technical experts, possibly from around the world, will help build a culture of effective response in the organization.

SUSTAINABLE

If the sales team needs to grow, loses talent, or needs to adjust strategy based on a change in business direction or philosophy, the company addresses those issues rapidly by hiring more people or reorganizing to avoid the risk of financial loss. When incident response passes the point of initial training and becomes a formal activity within an organization, the organization must view, care for, and value the Incident Response Team just like any other business unit.

Sustainability means that the incident response is indeed just as valuable as any other business unit, and deserves the same amount of financial commitment, executive leadership, and organizational development. Incident response in the IT field should not be viewed as a necessary evil, as we have seen in many organizations. Being on-duty to respond should be respected within the organization, intended to attract awesome and skilled talent. Incident response duty is painful sometimes—nobody likes to get up in the middle of the night on a regular basis—but this inconvenience is critical to the financial health and well-being of the company.

We say all this to underscore this point of sustainability. Few in the IT incident response business received any formal training on becoming an incident responder. Rather, individual technical skill or unique knowledge of an operating environment inadvertently leads them to the "tip of the spear" in incident response. Because a person may be a great engineer, they may be assigned to the Incident Response Team. Operations, specifically incident response as part of operations, is the place where technology and failure intersect, and the incident resolution process must be efficient to keep the business running. To that end, it is common to take great technical talent and bolt on incident response training, thus anointing the person as an incident responder, whether or not they are suited for the task. Many times, this approach works well and individuals make a smooth transition from technical expert to incident response technical expert, which are not necessarily the same thing. But many times, it simply does not work.

Again, establishing the culture of formalized incident response and looking after the team with support, leadership, and financial commitment will make attracting and keeping great talent a much easier task.

Summary

The goal of every business is to grow and create value. Every employee has a role and most spend their time building the business. Incident responders protect the business from the risks associated with service interruptions and outages. IT incident response is a specialized field in its own right and should be valued for its contributions to the long-term financial well-being of the company. The first step to building a successful incident management team is to conduct an honest assessment of the status quo. The following list of key points and concepts is a distillation of PROCESS in an easy-to-digest format:

- PROCESS is an acronym you can use as a programmatic evaluation tool. Using each point to guide a discussion about the various aspects of your incident response process can provide insights into areas you can improve.

- There should be no doubt about who is available to respond and who is available in the incident response talent pool.

- You should be able to respond the same way, every minute of every business hour.

- Team members should be trained, equipped, and ready to do the job the company is asking them to do.

- Everyone on the Incident Response Team should know exactly what is expected of them, what their role is, what latitude they have to make decisions on an incident, and know that they have support from executive leadership to resolve incidents to protect the business.

- Good incident response process can rapidly scale up and scale down to match the needs of the incident.

- Successful incident response programs are built to be sustainable in terms of recruiting and retaining the best talent.

- An organization should build and maintain a culture of incident response and view it as important as any other business unit.

- There is a difference between event, alert, incident, dispatch, and notification. If your company hasn't made that crystal clear to all responders and throughout the entire company, we suggest you do. We run into many companies that haven't done that and it creates confusion during the process of assembling the right team at the right time to do the right things.

2

The Incident Management System (IMS)

In 1970, a series of devastating wildfires swept across California, destroying more than 700 homes over 775 square miles in 13 days with 13 fatalities, and resulting in more than $233 million in losses (over $1 billion in today's dollars, adjusted for inflation). Thousands of firefighters from around the state and beyond responded, but found it very difficult to work together. They certainly knew how to fight fires, but lacked a common management framework that could scale up and down with the incident. They also lacked a standardized approach for incident leadership. Shortly thereafter, several fire service leaders created a revolutionary system for managing emergencies that range from the everyday fire and medical emergency to large-scale emergency events (such as the one depicted in Figure 2-1) that make the national news. The Incident Command System (ICS) was born, which has since evolved into the Incident Management System (IMS).

Figure 2-1. Forest fire. Credit: Jvdwolf (123RF.com)

The IMS was revolutionary because it cut across the geographical and cultural boundaries that separate fire departments. It offered a nondenominational platform that, in essence, served as an operating system for people within both a single fire department or when multiple fire departments needed to work together. And even though the core concepts of IMS seem simple and intuitive, adopting them wasn't without hardship because change isn't easy regardless of the company, profession, or industry.

The fire service, much like IT, has strong culture and strong opinions, and agreeing on *a way* of doing anything, much less adopting IMS as *the way of managing incidents*, was no easy feat. As a testament to how efficient and useful IMS is, it overcame all the political inertia and resistance to change that could have killed it off as a fad or "something that just won't work for us," as many fire departments are prone to say. Similarly, in IT, any company can argue that their environment, company size, or complexity is so unique as to preclude them from adopting IMS as a way to manage incidents.

IMS works because it is not like a set of rigid steps listed in a cookbook. Rather, it is a flexible, scalable approach baked into the culture of the company and the responders in order to provide the leadership and management to predictably and efficiently respond to all-hazard, all-risk events. It works in any IT environment.

You will see throughout the body of this book that we offer concepts and methods, aligned with common sense and intuition, for you to adopt in the quest for excellent incident management. You are free to pick and choose what works for you, including suggested job functions, terms, and definitions, or any other component of IMS. It took a catastrophic incident as a catalyst and 40 years of battle tested, daily use on incidents of all sizes and severity for IMS to become a national standard for the fire service. We don't expect it to be embraced overnight in IT, but we do say with confidence that it is a tried and true way to manage emergencies and it can work for you.

These are the most useful components of IMS that are directly applicable to IT:

- Provides a framework to manage and keep track of responders
- Establishes a single point of leadership
- Provides a platform to standardize job functions and terminology used by the responders

The goal of this chapter—and the entire book—is to provide an overview of IMS and its components, assist in translating the concepts to the IT world, and to help you build a reliable and organized IRT in your company.

You may not think that a building on fire and an IT incident have much in common, but from an IMS perspective, they are fundamentally similar. Both incidents may occur without warning. Both incidents are dynamic (i.e., both are in progress and not under control), create a negative impact of some type, and require a coordinated effort of the right people performing the right tasks at the right time to return systems to normal (i.e., a building that is not on fire or an IT environment that is not in an degraded state). The burning building and the IT incident both create *downtime* and the incident responders are there to return the situation to *uptime*.

In both situations, the first people who respond to the incident are "first responders." The response comes in the form of specially trained individuals or teams with not only technical skills, but also leadership skills and a management framework of organizing people into effective work groups. When working as an organized team under strong leadership, the incident resolvers with technical skills can assess a dynamic and evolving situation, develop plans to resolve the issue, communicate those plans, and work together to return to uptime in the shortest amount of time possible. To that end, there is a difference in *responding* to an incident and *reacting* to it. *Responders* are trained, organized, and disciplined in their approach to resolving an incident. They bring their experience and skill to the incident with focus and direction. *Reactors*, on the other hand, tend to be emotional and without discipline, either as individuals or a team. Each reactor generally has a different viewpoint on what's important to resolving the situation. There likely is no coordination among reactors, no recognition of the importance of a team, no delegation of tasks and sharing ideas or developing solutions in an organized fashion, and no focused effort of the group as whole.

Note

Responders are calm, cool, and collected and can think clearly under pressure. They arrive and direct the events that ultimately resolve an incident. Reactors get emotional and irrational and cannot stay focused or organized. They arrive and see an *emergency* not an incident. Which one are you?

Clearly, incident response is best accomplished by responders. Perhaps a good way to get your head around being one is by adapting this viewpoint from the fire service: "Fire is not an *emergency* to the fire department. It's what we do." When you dial 911 for the fire department, you expect a rapid response from a group of professionals, skilled in the art of solving whatever issue you are having on your "bad day." IT responders, regardless of whether they are using DevOps practices, ITIL, or homegrown systems, are similar to firefighters and should think of themselves in the same way. IT incident responders reduce the impact of an IT issue and restore the environment back to an acceptable state of operations.

Warning

Incident response is a people-to-people activity. The attitudes and demeanor of the people and how the work together as a team is vital.

To set the stage for anyone tasked with solving technology incidents, it is important to understand a fundamental concept: When an incident occurs, all individuals responsible for resolving the incident must shift his or her thinking and decision-making from *peacetime* to *wartime* and immediately transition from being a day-to-day technical resource working *for* the company, to being an incident responder tasked with *defending* the business. Make no mistake, downtime is an attack on your very livelihood, and the livelihood of everyone else in the company!

Peacetime is the steady-state environment of continuing operations that exists in nonincident mode. It's simple: peacetime is uptime.

Wartime is an urgent, degraded mode of operation that occurs when any application or infrastructure element experiences an issue outside the normal course of business. Wartime is downtime.

We've thought quite a lot about this peacetime/wartime analogy, and realize it might be viewed as excessive and/or may give an uneasy feeling about the connotation, but the important thing to focus on is that peacetime builds the business and wartime defends it. In *wartime*, the company is in downtime and its reputation, trust, and financial performance is at risk. Therefore, the people who respond to the IT incident must make a rapid change from their day-to-day job to being an incident responder.

This doesn't mean, however, that responders are frantic or hysterical. It means that the group understands the need to assemble quickly, get organized, stay on task, and get on with the business of resolution with urgency (not emergency!), and intensity. If you come from an agile development environment, think of incident response as a really fast and compressed sprint!

Having a responder (wartime) mentality, however, is just the tip of the iceberg when it comes to resolving IT incidents. An excellent group of technical experts without a strong leader and a framework to organize themselves cannot resolve incidents at maximum efficiency and minimum time. Conversely, strong leadership and a framework to organize people without the right technical expertise will not solve any issue quickly or efficiently. To that end, there must exist the right mix of expertise and leadership when it comes to resolving incidents.

Important to incident response is the use of monitoring and alerting tools for the technology stack, which provides the initial information for the responders and helps to size-up the incident and identify a severity (SEV) level. The SEV level is critical because it can be used to determine who initially responds to the incident and/or what type of subject matter expertise, such as network, database, or storage, might be needed to provide technical expertise.

Note

As with other terms used in this book, you may use a term other than SME to describe a technical expert or team of experts, or any other people or resource necessary to bring to an incident resolution. When we use the term SME, we are referring globally to a technical resource in a talent pool required to solve an IT incident.

One of the greatest assets to the leader of the incident resolution effort—the Incident Commander (IC)—is the subject matter expert (SME). The IC job function will be fleshed out in more detail throughout the remainder of the book, but for now, simply view that title as the top leader of the incident. As mentioned, IT systems are becoming so complex that it's virtually impossible for a single person to know everything about the whole stack and its operating environment, but even more importantly, how to fix all elements in that environment when they break. To that end, the person leading the incident response must rely on individual SMEs or teams by function (e.g., network, compute, storage, security, applications) to respond with urgency and with the right attitude, and to provide input and expertise within the framework of the IMS. If everyone knows and understands their role, and operates within the established system, the incident response will remain organized.

A good example of effective SME participation includes the following:

- Support the IC at all times (never let the IC fail!).

- Arrive on the bridge or respond to the incident as quickly as [possible.]

- Identify yourself by name and function when entering the incident communications channel. On a conference call bridge, you do this verbally. An example would sound like this, "Hi, this is Phillip, database." If using another communication method where you are asked to enter your name, type your actual name instead of "User 1." Being stealthy on the incident is not healthy! There is more about this in Chapter 3.

- Wait for a briefing or other instructions from the IC.

- Ensure that your work environment is quiet (no dogs barking in the background!).

- Speak up and speak clearly.

- Be specific and factual at all times.

- Respect the IC's timeline.

- Answer directly the probing questions you may be asked in order to come up with a realistic solution.

- Have backup plans in addition to your primary plan.

- If you need more help, ask for it.

"During my career," says Jason Tatem, lead engineer for site reliability at Salesforce, "I've had the opportunity to work closely with fire and police services. The change in organizational and individual posture when an incident starts is impressive to watch, and we've mirrored that in how we respond to incidents impacting our customers. To that end, it's important that boundaries between business units dissolve, and any asset, resource, or talent required to resolve the incident must be ready and able to assist until the incident is mitigated. Everyone refocuses and starts marching to the IC's beat," Tatem emphasizes. "All the individuals on the Incident Response Team know there is one focus—clear the incident." For certain, when an incident occurs and the team is assembled to resolve it, egos should be checked at the door. Incident response is a team sport!

In short, the process of IMS is about how your organization discovers an issue, how it dispatches the responders, how the IC organizes the responders, how those responders engage in the resolution effort, how escalations happen when more or different experts or outside vendors are needed, and how to control the communications channels and discussions when there are a lot of responders.

But having a good framework is only one part of efficient incident response. The next important ingredient is incident leadership and comes in the form of an Incident Commander (IC). Incident command is a *function* filled by a *person*, and that doesn't always have to be the same person. Many organizations rely on one or two people to be the designated ICs. This is because of the belief that the IC must be a senior executive or most technically proficient expert on the response.

Many organizations believe that a person's peacetime rank automatically carries over into wartime, but that is not always the case. We'll discuss this more throughout the book, but suffice it to say that the IC can be anyone in the organization, as long as they've been trained as an IC and can demonstrate competence. It's the IC's responsibility to lead the response and be proficient at setting up and managing the framework to keep the people moving forward with focus and a sense of urgency, irrespective of that person's rank or title in the organization.

Efficient incident response, then, is achieved by a scalable framework (IMS), plus leadership (IC), added to the appropriate problem solving talent (PS) and focused incident resolution required to bring the incident under control, all driven by the pressure of time to get back to uptime. Figure 2-2 captures this thought by way of a graphical representation.

$$\text{Efficient Incident Response} = \frac{(IMS + IC) + PS}{Time}$$

Figure 2-2. The efficient incident response formula

Remove any one of these elements (except the time pressure, of course), and the overall incident resolution effort will be less effective than it could be. For example, weak or absent incident leadership allows for chaos on the incident conference call bridge. A lack of framework, or the inability to scale as more incident responders are needed, also leads to chaos and conflict. The wrong mix of personalities and expertise trying to solve a significant issue is also a pathway to inefficiency. Chaos adds complexity and frustration, but more importantly, adds unnecessary time to the incident resolution, elongating mean time to repair (MTTR) and putting the company's business at greater risk. Anyone who has led or participated in an incident response with ego-driven individuals, the wrong type of expertise, or SMEs that don't understand why they were called in the first place, knows that these can be significant obstacles when it comes to resolving incidents. Time is added to the equation because without speed and efficiency, time is wasted.

Note

Time is the one resource you can never get back! Time can't be created. It can only be saved or wasted.

Generally, the talent required to solve IT incidents exists within the organization. Leadership of incident responders can be trained, developed, and exercised until it is done with speed and ease. Much like ITIL is intended to be a best practice to align IT services with business functions, IMS is a best practice to align incident response functions for restoring uptime.

Overview of Incident Command

Without leadership and a process to organize and direct personnel and resources, the effort to resolve an incident may end up being as complicated and uncertain as the issue itself. Therefore, for any incident to be successfully managed, there must be only one person in charge—the Incident Commander (Figure 2-3).

Figure 2-3. The only person in charge of an incident response should be the Incident Commander

Note

IMS uses the term Incident Commander (IC) to identify the function of incident leadership. We recognize that your incident response system may use a different term such as incident owner (IO), incident manager (IM), technical lead, or lead engineer. We prefer the term Incident Commander, and will use it throughout this book.

The IC should:

- Ensure that the responders have a clear understanding of the issue. The IC doesn't need to be the best technical expert, but must be skilled at moving the incident forward with purpose and direction.

- Set clear incident resolution objectives.

- Work with SMEs to interpret key metrics from monitoring tools and facilitate a discussion aimed at building an incident action plan (and a backup plan if appropriate).

- Keep an eye on the clock and keep the resolution effort on track and moving forward.

- Have access to whatever pool of resources, inside or outside the company, is required to resolve the incident.

- Establish reliable methods to communicate across the various disciplines handling the incident.

- Provide information to key players in a timely manner.

Aside from organizing the responders, an IC may field questions from executives regarding estimated downtime, update internal communications, survey customer experience, and release personnel from the incident when appropriate so they can return to their peacetime job. These are very real demands made by others who may or may not appreciate the complexity of managing an incident.

A large part of being a good IC is keeping the participants focused on incident response objectives. Minutes can turn into hours when the incident conference call bridge becomes an off-topic committee meeting or finger-pointing exercise and not a resolution-oriented, mission-critical, resolution effort.

How does all this happen?

Essentially it all boils down to good leadership, fact-based decision-making, forward thinking, and teamwork. "The hardest part of an Incident Commander's job, from my experience," says Morgan Collins, IC and senior manager of North American site reliability at Salesforce, "is understanding the necessity of taking high-risk actions and being ready to build from a failed action. The needs of the customer, company, and internal personnel engaged on an incident are fulfilled by action and the ability to guide through an adverse situation. Failure generates data. Hesitation by an Incident Commander generates doubt, fear, and uncertainty."

The Culture of Incident Response

Progressive organizations recognize that failures in their IT environment will occur. They understand that they operate large, complex systems and build in redundancy and resiliency to maximize uptime, but they also understand that failures will still occur. Failure creates downtime and as we've said, downtime equals wartime. Highly mature organizations will create teams of incident responders to operate specifically in wartime. These organizations have two very different organization charts: one for peacetime and one for wartime (see Figure 2-4). The peacetime org chart is the usual org chart of business, with a CEO, COO, and functional heads of Marketing, Sales, Engineering, and Operations teams. The wartime org chart has the IC at the top, with the SMEs and other key incident resolvers listed by function.

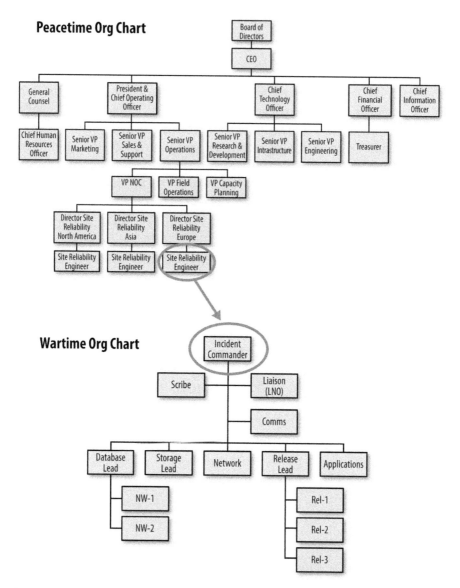

Figure 2-4. Peacetime and wartime org charts

The wartime organizational chart will not look the same as the peacetime organizational chart. What the org charts don't illustrate is the way that people relate to each other, the differences in how decisions get made, and the urgency behind the speed at which tasks are carried out. Many organizations conduct nonincident (peacetime) business under a consensus-based culture, focused on soliciting input from various stakeholders to collaborate and execute a corporate vision. Peacetime leaders are typically focused on the business of running the company to achieve the corporate goals of growing revenue, increasing earnings, and creating value. In peacetime, making a highly optimized decision is very important, whereas in wartime, making the best decision in the shortest amount of time is the goal.

All organizations have internal politics to some degree, and it is not uncommon for small fiefdoms to exist. Practically speaking, organizations large and small have a "way things are done around here," and in many cases, those practices and principles are at cross-purposes to managing and leading incidents, mostly as it relates to sharing or supplying vital talent to the response. Once IMS is adopted into the existing "way things work" culture, certain challenges to the organization's culture of incident response may emerge. Those challenges could include the following:

- Talent required to resolve an incident comes from business units not directly under the control of the IC and ultimately the IC may need to solicit, procure, task, and maintain control of talent owned by another group or division with competing interests.

- Outside vendors may play a role in incident resolution. They may have a revolving talent pool because they are balancing staffing with service level agreements (SLAs) required by contractual obligations, which creates issues in deploying a consistent response. The success of IMS is partly based on a PROCESS response with resources that understand the IMS process.

- Executive leadership joins an incident conference call bridge and engages in the response, but likely not with the same level of technical expertise as the Incident Response Team. Many executives bring their peacetime rank to the wartime incident, potentially intimidating other responders of lesser peacetime rank. Executives also may feel the need to demonstrate leadership even when they may not have the IC leadership skills or be the most technically proficient expert.

IMS is a way upon which an IT organization can build its incident operations doctrine. In other words, adopting the principles and practices set forth in

IMS can become *the way* for an IT organization just as it did in the fire service. Examples of the elements that form the basis of an organization's operational doctrine (how we respond) include:

- Establishing and enforcing incident response time standards, such as service level agreements (SLAs) for SMEs or other resources.

- Selecting who fills the role of IC.

- Defining how the incident response process interacts with internal and external stakeholders. This includes specifically identifying how key peacetime leadership is notified, how they are kept up-to-date, and how they participate on an incident conference call bridge.

- Establishing levels of severity (SEV) in order to have a common operating picture of the impact of the incident.

- Setting the path for how the technical experts (SMEs) enter the incident and interact with the IC and fellow responders.

- Developing the people-to-people skills of an IC in order to be better leaders during an incident.

- Establishing methods and implementing best practices to make thoughtful and technically sound decisions.

Note

The culture of the organization should support IMS. Anyone who might be called on to respond to an incident should understand his or her role.

For incident response to be successful, any company adopting IMS should conduct IMS training across its workforce. This ensures consistency in incident response and begins to ingrain IMS into the culture of the company. Incident management is a specialized discipline of operations and should be recognized by the organization for the important role that it plays in the company's success. In this fast-paced world, incident resolution decisions must be made at the same pace as the incident is unfolding. To that end, teamwork, effective communications, and information stewardship are key.

Key resources in an organization should be immediately available to the IRT, and the IC must be able to reach across traditional organizational boundaries in order to use all the talent available to resolve the incident. Everyone on the Incident Response Team reports to the IC, even if during peacetime these are people several pay grades or levels above the IC, or executives in another division who are on the bridge.

This book is only a single step in the process of becoming an incident responder. You already have the required technical expertise and experience for problem-solving. Using IMS will help you understand how to organize and deliver that expertise in a structured and coordinated manner.

Additionally, this book is designed to be conceptual in nature for one very important reason—incidents are potentially so diverse that it would be impossible to cover all scenarios or give a step-by-step guide for every potential situation. Plus, each company architects, implements, and operates its technology stack differently. Organizations utilize human resources in so many different ways that it's impossible for us to offer a "one size fits all" approach. Rather, our goal is to translate the broad concepts of IMS from the US fire service into IT operations and leave it up to you to interpret and adopt what works for your circumstance. This approach allows the IRT to become more of an all-hazard, all-risk set of responders, able to adapt to most any type of incident.

Ultimately, this text is aimed at providing you with a toolbox for building an incident response program as well as effectively managing an incident. You will then be able to remove as many tools from your toolbox as necessary to solve whatever situation you are facing. IMS expands and contracts to meet the needs of the situation, and it doesn't care what you are trying to handle.

COMMON TERMINOLOGY FOR JOB FUNCTIONS

Another important IMS concept is the use of standardized language across the IRT to drive effective communications. IT, like many other industries, is full of jargon, acronyms, abbreviations, and technical terms. These acronyms and abbreviations are used to shorten the time of communications. For example, AWS is used instead of Amazon Web Services and DBA is used instead of database administrator. Without common terminology, the very tool for shortened communications (acronyms and abbreviations) could actually slow down communications significantly. There is a possibility that different words or acronyms will mean different things to different people and may result in not everyone on the incident conference bridge understanding 100% of the discussion. This is important because without a common communication system using common terminology, the incident will be destined for failure. This common terminology —mostly as it relates to job functions—will be discussed later in the document.

To illustrate the point, let's look at the term Emergency Medical Technician and its acronym EMT, which is a common job function and acronym used in the emergency medical services field. Here's just a few things EMT could possibly represent, depending on the audience:

- Emergency Medical Technician
- Emergency Management Team
- Eastern Mediterranean Time (GMT+0200)
- El Monte, CA (airport code)
- Electron Microscope Tomography
- E-mail Money Transfer

So, if someone has a broken leg, they need an Emergency Medical Technician, not an E-mail Money Transfer! Like EMT, the term IC has different meanings to different people. The IC (Incident Commander—not individual contributor, a term used in some organizations) should be leading a group that completely understands the technical jargon, acronyms, and abbreviations of your environment and the incident. Further, all incident responders must understand the language of IMS. It matters less what you call a group or job function as long as everyone throughout the organization shares the same understanding.

This section presents descriptions of some commonly used incident response terms and job functions found in IMS. You can certainly change the names to better fit your organization. We are only offering them as suggested functional positions that may assist you in organizing your response. *The one name that shouldn't change is the Incident Commander (IC) because when you have an incident, it needs to be commanded—not managed or owned!*

Again, based on the size of your company or number of incident responders that might typically respond, you might not need to use all the functions listed, or you may have others not listed here. The beauty of IMS is that it's totally fine to customize the system to your operations. As long as its fully understood by everyone, you can use the system in a way that fits the organization (remember PROCESS!). The key is to establish the positions and use terminology that is appropriate and clearly understood in your operating environment. Some of these job functions will be explained in more detail as you work your way through the rest of the book.

Incident Commander (IC)

The leader of the incident response is responsible for focusing the group, developing incident objectives, providing direction and time management. The IC may or may not be the person that initially establishes the incident bridge, and may not be the most senior person in the peacetime org chart. Also, it is not necessary for the IC to be the deepest technical expert in the area in which the incident is occurring. It may be helpful, but can also be a detriment. For example, an IC with specific technical domain expertise, such as network, may have a tendency to act as a network SME (begin working directly on the incident resolution) rather than function in the role of IC. *The IC must be an expert in the process and function of incident command—this is the most important thing to keep in mind!* The IC shall remain the IC for the duration of the event or until command is transferred to another IC. Formal transfer of command information should be exchanged prior to the new IC taking charge.

Communications Officer (Comms)

This job function is responsible for all incident responder notifications and may also assist the IC with issuing executive briefings or stakeholder notifications. When the IC needs to reach an SME or executive, the Comms Officer should be tasked with making the notifications.

Group Leader

This job function is created by the IC to lead a group of SMEs from similar functions or other resources. For example, if three DBAs respond to the incident conference call bridge, the IC can appoint one DBA as the DBA group leader, who will then lead the other DBAs and report directly to the IC. There is more on this position in Chapter 6.

Situational Status (SitStat)

Also known as the scribe, this is the person who records all of the information related to the incident. They are responsible for keeping track of the Situational Status (SitStat), updating technical briefs or other forms of incident documentation.

Plans Group (Plans)

This is a group established by the IC on large-scale or complex incidents and does not need to reside within the technical Operations Team. The Plans group is comprised of SMEs who are thinking about alternative resolution options to the current incident action plan (Plan A). Plans listens to the activity and war-games alternative plans and contingencies. Plans does not actively participate in the Plan A development. Plans is responsible for developing Plan B, C, D, and beyond, and identifying the advantages/disadvantages of each plan.

Subject Matter Expert (SME)

This job function is the technical experts supporting and working with the IC, even if during peacetime operations the SME may be the supervisor of the IC. The SME population will vary from company to company and may be a globally distributed workforce. In larger companies with complex environments, SMEs called to an incident conference call bridge may be many time zones away and not personally acquainted with the IC or anyone else on the incident bridge.

Summary

A best practice for the IT industry exists outside the IT industry. Incident management is a critical part of providing highly reliable IT services and the best practices for incident management has been battle-tested in the US fire service since the development of IMS in 1970. The Incident Management System (IMS) is an all-hazard, all-risk framework designed specifically for emergency operations. The Incident Commander (IC) leads the Incident Response Team (IRT) using the principle of IMS.

- When an incident occurs, all individuals responsible for resolving the incident must immediately shift his or her thinking, decision-making, and operational posture from peacetime to wartime.

- Solving wartime incidents requires a wartime mentality, behavioral patterns, and organizational structure. The IMS is the framework that organizes a pool of SMEs under the leadership of the IC in order to form a collaborative and cohesive incident response effort.

- The first key principle of incident response, and the cornerstone of the IMS, is that every incident response must have leadership. Not every event such as a trouble ticket or low-severity event requires an IC, but a true incident must have a person leading the response.

- In incident response, everyone must work together for the system to work.

- The overall goal of incident response is to resolve the incident as quickly and efficiently as possible in order to return the operations of the company to a business-as-usual or peacetime state, and protect the company's reputation, trust with customers, confidence with investors, and financial results.

- There are many possible job functions that could be established by an IRT. It's up to you to customize IMS to fit your need.

3

The Incident Commander (IC)

Readers who've been working in IT operations roles may have participated in many incidents as a responder, but may or may not have had the opportunity to lead an incident. If you have had the pleasure, you know it can be a stressful and overwhelming endeavor. If you haven't, there will likely come a day when you'll be called upon to do so. Leading an incident is challenging and mentally taxing, especially in situations where the solution to the issue isn't obvious, the pressure is on, and time is ticking away.

Dealing with the multitude of personalities both on and off the incident conference call bridge can be as challenging as figuring out the solution to a tough technical issue. Some people may question or criticize your decisions while others openly praise your leadership. Your actions may be quietly, or, in some cases, not so quietly, second-guessed. After the incident is over and the cause of it becomes clear, some may question why it took so long to resolve. Of course, if you had all the answers at the beginning of an incident that you do at the end, you may have made different decisions.

Ultimately, you will earn some sort of reputation as an Incident Commander (IC; Figure 3-1). It may be good or bad, but it will certainly follow you as well as precede you to every incident response you lead. It is therefore critical that you and your IRT start with a solid foundation and adopt a few key principles.

Figure 3-1. Just like a fire department Incident Commander, it is your job to grab hold of the turbulence during the response and direct it toward a realistic endpoint

First and foremost, when you are the IC, it's important that your actions and behaviors inspire confidence. You may facilitate and encourage discussion, but it is done from the viewpoint as the leader, using a variety of interpersonal skills (active listening, task assignment to named resources, time management, etc.) to direct the effort. This posture of firm, directed, and clear leadership is referred to as *command presence*. In short, command presence is the ability to convey to your followers that you are in charge and capable of leading. Coined by the military to express the qualities of a person that leads troops in combat, command presence is hard to define in words, but you certainly know it when you see it. Anyone reading this book has run across great and poor leaders in their professional career, and it's clear to see the distinction between the two. We can't teach command presence in a textbook. It's developed through training, exercises, continuous practice, trial and error, and leading incidents. When you find your groove as a leader, you can feel it and so can the followers. We will offer some tips and advice, but the rest is up to you!

You should use IMS as a framework to organize personnel, but keep in mind that IMS is a tool for management—not a substitute for leadership. There is a simple and clear distinction between management and leadership, and it is important to understand: *Things are managed, people are led. For example, a budget is a thing and it's managed but a team is a group of people and they're led.*

The IC sets the tone for the incident. When the IC is calm, cool, collected, and focused, it sets the atmosphere for all other incident responders. Good ICs are assertive but also know how to identify and work with a variety of personality traits to achieve maximum results. Good ICs are impartial and not emotionally attached to their own position or viewpoint. The IC must be open to all input and stay focused on leading the group toward the best and most efficient approach to resolving the incident. Nick Ravenhall, senior manager of site reliability at Salesforce in Dublin, Ireland says, "The Incident Commander is a critical position no matter what the size of the incident, but, as the severity of the incident increases, so does the level of pressure. All members of the resolution team are looking to you for guidance, direction, decision-making, a sense of urgency, and—above all —calmness. For me, it always came down to two things: the trust I had in my subject matter experts to provide me with all of the relevant information and the confidence that I had in my own ability to make the right calls at the right times."

Many new ICs become overwhelmed with all the decisions that need to be made and risk falling into common traps—from having an opinion on everything (micromanaging) to allowing the group to hash out a solution on an uncertain timeline (schedule creep).

Note

A good IC can gather information in the present and predict how it will behave in the future.

The IC should be so focused on their role directing the incident *resolution effort* they should have no bandwidth left to get into the physical act of typing on a keyboard themselves to solve the issue. To explain this concept more fully, here are a few frequently asked questions about incident command:

QUESTION: I am identified as one of the qualified Incident Commanders for my shift, but I also have experience and expertise as a database administrator (aka DBA SME). If an incident occurs and the issue is clearly within our database, should I work on solving this database issue myself or be the Incident Commander for our IRT?

ANSWER: You don't have to be a technical expert in the affected area to be the Incident Commander. It may be helpful to have a working knowledge of the affected systems, provided you don't lose perspective and start problem solving instead of commanding, but it's not required. To effectively lead the incident, step out of your engineer (SME) role and step into the Incident Commander role. The Incident Commander must be skilled in using the IMS framework to organize and lead the team, whereas SMEs are experts in their respective technical domains. If you assume the role of Incident Commander, then you should perform the IC function or pass it to someone else.

QUESTION: I am the Incident Commander. Do I have to make all the decisions?

ANSWER: The Incident Commander is ultimately responsible for all the decisions made but does not have to make all of them. A good IC will create an environment of lively and open discussion among the right mix of SMEs. The goal is to draw information out of the technical experts to understand the issue and then formulate a plan of attack to solve it. The IC should not be a heavy-handed dictator that directs each and every move on the incident conference call bridge. Rather, the IC is there to work with the entire team, distill the information into a useful plan, keep the response focused and moving forward, and declare an endpoint when the incident is resolved.

QUESTION: I am a senior executive in the organization during peacetime. Should I always be the Incident Commander?

ANSWER: No. Incident command is a function and the position can be filled by anyone who is qualified to fill it. The IC needs to be excellent at leading the response, and that does not always correlate to seniority or rank or title within the peacetime organization. The owner of a baseball team doesn't come onto the field to pinch hit in the bottom of the ninth inning when the game is on the line. The players were hired to play the game. The owner's job revolves around managing the business of the game. The players are responsible for playing it at all times and in all circumstances.

Resolving the Incident

"So how do we fix this?"

This is an easy question to ask but sometimes a difficult one to answer, especially when systems are down, customers are impacted, and there is no clear-cut solution readily available. The executive leadership is concerned with the possible negative financial impact to the business, erosion of customer trust, damage to the organization's reputation, and loss of confidence by investors. It's even more difficult when all eyes are on you and the stress level of those asking the question is rising. A good IC should be like a duck swimming on the smooth surface of a lake. Above the water, the duck appears serene and moving almost without effort. Below the surface of the water the duck is paddling like crazy! And so goes the life of an IC—calm and cool on the outside while his or her brain is working at a fevered pitch on the inside. Calmness in the IC instills calmness in others, just as out-of-control excitement breeds the same thing among the incident responders. As the IC goes, so goes the environment on the incident conference bridge or your chosen method of incident communication!

The IC must be aware of what is currently going on with the incident but also must be continually thinking about the next move(s). The IC should be working with the SMEs to determine a sound plan for incident resolution, as well as prompting the group to think about alternative plans. During high-severity (SEV) incidents, it is usually a struggle to develop a good first plan to resolve an issue. Nonetheless, the Incident Commander must also get the group thinking about an alternative plan (plan B) and possibly multiple additional plans (plans C, D, E, etc.) if warranted. For example, if the SMEs have offered a solution to the issue and the IC approves the plan, the next words from the Incident Commander should be "Let's discuss alternative plans (plan B)," even while the SMEs are implementing plan A.

As with other responsibilities, the IC is responsible for thinking about these alternative plans but does not have to develop these plans alone, especially if the IC is not an expert in the affected area. If there are enough responders working the issue, the IC can assign a few SMEs to a planning (Plans) group (refer back to Chapter 2 for this job function description). This group might assemble on another communications platform (for example, a separate conference bridge or chat group), give some thought to other ways to resolve the incident, and report their progress back to the Incident Commander on the main incident conference bridge.

ICs should always ask the following questions when thinking about alternative plans:

- Regarding the current plan, what are key indicators that the plan is working or not working?

- What is the trigger point to abandon the initial plan and move to the next one?

- Will I need more or different technical talent (SMEs) to implement an alternative plan?

- How will I communicate to the IRT to abandon the current plan and move to an alternative plan?

As previously mentioned, it is the role of the IC to set the tone for the incident and approve the actions to be taken but leave it to the SMEs to execute the specific actions. In some cases, the IC may need or want to hear the SMEs debate the pros and cons of a solution. As a solution is proposed by one or more SME groups, the IC should then ask each SME whether they support the plan or not. This gives each SME an opportunity to agree or disagree with the proposed solution. The IC is looking for support, not consensus. *This isn't about power or control. It's about having a single person summarize, consolidate, and ensure understanding across the entire group of incident responders. At the end, the Incident Commander will make the final call.*

Note

A good IC isn't concerned about making a quick decision. The goal is to make the best decision in the shortest amount of time.

Once the IRT understands the issue and has a plan with a reasonable chance of success, the issue becomes one of time management and marching forward toward incident resolution. ICs should know that the pressure of time is the constant friend and enemy of the incident response. It is a friend when a good leader uses it to keep SMEs focused by assigning tasks and providing specific direction with clear time frames, and then holding them responsible and accountable to that time frame. It is the enemy when minutes turn to hours with unproductive conversations or actions taking place on the incident conference bridge, such as when an unfocused group engages in free-for-all conversations that have no bearing on the incident or solution, or when one or more individuals try to prove who is the smartest person in the room. These kinds of behaviors steal precious time that can never be recovered. The Incident Commander must control the environment and influence the time it takes to resolve an incident.

Here is a typical conversation we hear on incident conference call bridges:

"I think we might we have a performance degradation on node 1. Can somebody figure that out?"

After a brief pause, a response from an unidentified voice: "Uh sure, I'll take a look."

Compare that conversation with this example of crisp and direct communication taking place on a conference call bridge:

Incident Commander: "Network, we have performance degradation on node 1. Can you go off the bridge, take a look at your monitoring tools, and get back to me in 10 minutes?"

Network: "Copy that, go off the bridge to look at the performance degradation on node 1 and get back to you in 10 minutes."

The differences are clear. One method tends to be nonspecific and meandering whereas the other is more direct and to the point.

Which type of conversation do you typically hear during your incidents?

You will also notice we use words and phrases commonly used in public safety, such as "copy" as a way to convey that you received and understood a written or verbal communication. We realize that using these terms may not appeal to all incident responders, but clear, crisp, and concise communication is vital, however you choose to do it.

To that end, ICs should get into the habit of following communication protocols. Let's use the preceding example for illustration:

- Identify a specific person (by name or function), instead of tossing out a vague question to a group and hoping that "somebody" takes on the task.

    — "Network"

- Make an assignment: clearly state the objective of the task, request, or action along with a specific time frame to complete it.

    — "We have a performance degradation on node 1. Can you go off the bridge, take a look at your monitoring tools, and get back to me in 10 minutes?"

- Expect the receiver of the task to acknowledge and repeat back a summary of the assignment.

    — "Copy that, go off the bridge to look at the performance degradation on node 1 and get back to you in 10 minutes."

That exchange was clear, crisp and concise, yet only took a few seconds to complete. The benefit of these types of wartime communications is that they save time. If the Incident Commander can save a few seconds on each conversation with SMEs, then the entire IRT can pick up otherwise wasted minutes and reduce the overall MTTR.

Clear and direct communications (both written and verbal) as well as time-based tasking during an incident will help ensure that people are working on the timeline established by the IC instead of allowing the response to meander aimlessly around the issue. Figure 3-2 shows some common communications tools used in incident response. The IC must clearly outline expectations in order for the SMEs to meet those expectations.

Figure 3-2. A speakerphone is commonly used for conference call incident bridges; use it like the public safety radio on the right

COMMUNICATION METHODS

If you conduct incident response efforts on a conference call bridge, you have a wide-open channel for communications. This means that everyone who dialed into the bridge has equal access to the main communication channel. This can be challenging to the IC, as it requires thoughtful and assertive action to reduce unproductive chatter and control the conversation. To that end, when operating on an incident bridge, the IC should be aware of the different ways to communicate.

Incident Commander to single resource (SME)

This is conducted much like a radio transmission that you would hear on a fire department radio channel. See Figure 3-3.

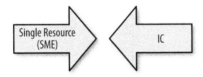

Figure 3-3. Incident Commander to single resource (SME) communication

The IC isolates a person or group by name and stops all other conversations on the bridge. The exchange is carried out as long as needed, and the IC may choose to put others on standby if they try to get airtime. An example looks like this:

Incident Commander: "Network, we have performance degradation on node 1. Can you go off the bridge, take a look at your monitoring tools, and get back to me in 10 minutes?"

Database: "Hey, I was just looking at the change cases from a couple of days ago."

Incident Commander: "Database, stand by."

Database: "Copy, database standing by."

Network: "Incident Commander, this is network, going off the bridge to look at the performance degradation on node 1 and get back to you in 10 minutes."

Incident Commander: "Okay, database, go ahead."

Database: "Yeah, I was looking at the change cases from a couple of days ago and it looks like we had a similar issue. Not sure if this is the same thing or not."

Incident Commander: "Database, good to know. Can you check your logs and get back to me in five minutes? Let's see what network comes up with."

Incident Commander to group

This form of communication is useful when an IC needs to provide a general briefing to the group, refocus a discussion, offer a general thought, or ask a question. See Figure 3-4.

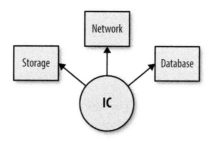

Figure 3-4. Incident Commander to group communication

The goal is to disseminate information or stimulate general discussion/ thinking among all participants on the incident bridge.

The following is a simple depiction of the conversation flow and certainly could involve a much bigger audience or be more complex:

Incident Commander: "Okay everyone, listen up. We've been at this for about 27 minutes and, as I understand it, we have narrowed down the issue to a service disruption on node 1. Network has looked at it and is certain that there's an issue with a load balancer. We should be able to resolve this within the next 15 minutes. Is anyone aware of any issues with this plan?

IC waits for a few seconds

Incident Commander: "Hearing no issues, I want to keep everyone on the bridge for now until we are certain of the fix. While we are waiting to see if this resolves the issue, I want to discuss what our plan B will be if this approach fails to resolve the situation."

In this example, the IC gained control of the bridge, summarized the current status, and provided the group with an informational report. Frequently and/or when significant new information is discovered, the IC should summarize the current situation and provide a CAN report to ensure clarity among all responders.

CAN is an acronym for *conditions, actions, needs* and is an easy way to remember the process for giving a quick, concise briefing. *Conditions* means the current status; *actions* are what is being done; and *needs* includes any additional resources or actions that are needed—usually in the form of people, time, or tasks.

The CAN report is a way to distill a message down into its most basic parts in the following circumstances:

- When new incident responders enter the conversation
- When the IC needs to brief key executives, vendors, or customers
- When the IC needs to refocus the group

Let's put the IC's briefing in the CAN report format for clarity:

Conditions

> "Okay, everyone listen up. We've been at this for about 27 minutes and as I understand it, we have narrowed down the issue to a service disruption on node 1."

Actions

> "Network has looked at it and is certain it's a load balancer. We should be able to resolve this within the next 15 minutes."

Needs

> "I want to keep everyone on the bridge for now until we are certain of the fix. While we are waiting to see if this resolves the issue, I want to discuss what our plan B will be if this action fails to resolve this incident."

In this exchange, the IC directed an SME (network) to carry out a task and gave a time horizon. Assigning a time limit to critical tasks puts the recipient of the task under time pressure, provides accountability, and keeps incident resolution moving forward. If the IC leaves the task open-ended, there is no expectation for performance and the SME may not appreciate the urgency in the same way that the IC does. Also, in this example, the SME confirmed the task by repeating the directive, thereby ensuring that both the IC and SME understood the task—a very good habit to get into when it comes to speaking the language of incident response.

That exchange was clear, crisp, and concise, yet only took a few seconds to complete. The benefit of these types of wartime communications is that they save time. If the IC can save a few seconds on each conversation with SMEs, then the entire IRT can pick up otherwise wasted minutes and reduce the overall MTTR.

SME to SME, or group discussion

This is used when the IC has an interest in soliciting opinions, support, or discussion among the group on the bridge. The IC presides over the discussion, guiding it to flow in a productive way. When this form of communication is used, the IC wants to *hear the thinking process* of a group of SMEs, such as a group of database administrators (DBAs) thinking through the possible reasons for an issue. This is useful when a brainstorming session is needed and the thought processes are useful for all (including the IC) to hear.

This is different than asking a single SME a question and simply receiving an answer from that person. In that form of communication, all the experience and knowledge gets processed internally in the head of the SME and only the answer is articulated. If there is a high level of trust in the SME or the SME has very specific knowledge in a particular area, perhaps the IC may simply ask a question and receive the answer. When the IC finds it useful for a discussion to take place for the benefit of the entire group, the IC may issue a directive such as the one illustrated in Figure 3-5. The figure shows the elements of a discussion (moderated by the IC) in order to reach the requested conclusion in the folowing narrative:

Incident Commander: "Okay, looks like I have four DBAs on the line. I'm going to create a database group and appoint John Smith as the Database Group Leader. Database group, you have 10 minutes to think through why we have 10 customers that can't access their data. Node 1 is involved, and I'm trying to understand what could possibly be the cause."

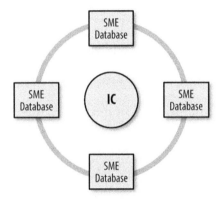

Figure 3-5. SME to SME, or group communication

If a broader, more open forum is warranted, the IC may open the discussion to all participants or perhaps a larger, heterogeneous group. Figure 3-6 depicts that process. Imagine the IC allowing and presiding over a free discussion (within the boundaries set by the IC, of course). The danger here is that the discussion gets bogged down or off topic and the IC might have to reign in the participants, which is done by the IC giving a CAN report to refocus the conversation. If free flowing discussion is warranted, the IC should lay down some ground rules prior to starting. It may sound something like this:

Incident Commander: "Okay, I've got several DBAs on the line, a couple of SAN engineers, an application manager, and one of our outside vendors.

We still haven't isolated the cause of the performance degradation on node 1. We've been at this for over 60 minutes and I'm concerned that we haven't made any real progress in terms of understanding the issue. I'm opening the floor to discussion and nothing is off the table in terms of possible causes. I want to hear from everyone on this and I'll take notes on what you come up with. We have 10 minutes, starting now."

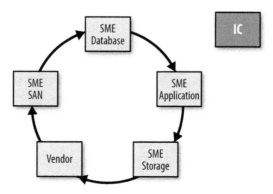

Figure 3-6. Opening up the group discussion to a more heterogeneous group when necessary

In order to facilitate these types of discussions, the Incident Commander must be an attentive and active listener, and carefully control the flow and tempo of the interactions. Multitasking may sound like a good idea, but during an incident it rarely yields the same results as focused efforts. In reality, controlling the chaos of a bridge requires the focused attention of the IC, and even a subtle deviation in the process can throw the entire incident response off track and consume valuable time.

- Listen for tone, inflection, and meaning, not just the actual words that are said. If the incident responders sound tired or frustrated, or there is confrontation between SMEs, stop the conversation immediately and refocus the discussion.

- Don't just wait for your turn to talk. Listen to the discussion and interpret the information being presented. Don't just focus on the general concepts people outline; focus on what they are saying and how they are saying it. Are they confident or are they just randomly throwing ideas out?

- Clarify the discussion. It's always good to periodically stop the action and summarize the progress, which the IC does by giving a CAN report and refocusing the discussion. This allows the incident responders to take a quick mental break and brings everyone back to a common point.

- Listen for those who are *NOT* contributing or who are being talked over by stronger voices. Some people may not be assertive, so the IC may have to clear the air for them and give them the floor, regardless of what communications channels are used to manage the incident.

Today, there are many types of communications methods (voice, text, video) and a wide variety of communications tools (conference bridges, IRC, SMS, email, Skype, FaceTime, WebEx, Slack, HipChat) and undoubtedly there will be more developed in the future. We are strong advocates for methods that come closest to actual human-to-human communications. Clearly, getting the IC and the entire IRT in one conference room would be optimal, but given the nature of distributed global teams, that is virtually impossible. The next best is video communications, but those tools may be distracting to many. Voice communications are next on the list. Text based is last on our list.

As you can see from the preceding list, it's not just the content of the conversation, but for the Incident Commander, it's more about the human emotions (confidence, hesitation, fear, uncertainty, conviction) conveyed in the conversation. Those subtle emotions are critical to understanding the meaning behind the words of the technical solutions presented. It's a key responsibility of the IC to be an active listener of the discussion and test the certainty and conviction of SMEs, especially when the issue doesn't have a clear path to resolution. If an IC asks a question and hears "um" or "well" or "ah, gee" from an SME, that's a red flag to the IC and should lead to more detailed questions. As humans, we unconsciously react with words and body language that expose our true intent, which may be different than the words we say. Picking up on those subtle clues is a really critical part of the IC's job. Audio conference call bridges are certainly not perfect, but the IC can hear those human emotions. Unfortunately, text-based communications tools can't convey those subtle clues in the same way that voice tools can.

Developing the Incident Action Plan

No matter what type of incident is occurring, there are certain objectives that should be met during the Incident Lifecycle. These are the milestones of the incident response and they are achieved by good decision-making and group dynamics facilitated by the IC. There are four key milestones that an IC should address when directing the response, which can be remembered by using the mnemonic STAR.

STAR stands for: *size up* the issue; perform *triage* to determine the severity; develop an *action* plan and resolve the issue, and *review*.

Regardless of the nature of the incident, it is important to take time to understand the issue or at least the presence of an incident, not an event, outside normal operations, as early as possible. This investigation ultimately results in the decision to make the transition from peacetime to wartime and to assign a severity level to the incident. From that point on, if the glass on the fire alarm is broken and the handle pulled, it's go time for the incident responders.

SIZE UP THE INCIDENT

No matter what the issue is, it is the responsibility of the IC (and the entire IRT for that matter) to get as much information as possible and to truly understand the nature of the incident. There is no shortage of monitoring tools available, each having its own merit and usefulness, which can provide data for the IRT to consider when assessing the situation. It is important to not only know that an incident exists, but more importantly, to understand *what* is happening. Getting oriented to the battle is about gaining *situational awareness* (SA). *SA* is about focus and observation. It's about understanding the visual, verbal, and technology cues available, orienting yourself—and perhaps other incident responders—to inputs relative to the current situation, and making sound decisions based on those inputs. SA provides the basis for the conditions part of the CAN report.

Think about it this way: decision-making and leadership are people-to-people activities. To that end, SA is a continuous process of human focus and observation of the data inputs. With all the monitoring tools available on the market, making decisions based on verifiable inputs is more common than ever in IT incident response.

Note

Monitoring tools provide data. Humans use judgment to make decisions.

When military fighter pilots talk about SA, they describe an ability to "get ahead of the airplane," which is good, and, if all things are going well, to "stay ahead of the airplane," which is even better. Nothing is worse than playing catch-up when you're trying to manage an incident. The same holds true for incident responders. Using monitoring tools and resources, coupled with clear thinking and good communication between the incident responders, helps the group keep pace with events and clearly understand the situation.

Initial actions

Without accurately identifying the issue, you are basing your decisions on anecdotal information, speculation, and luck. The following list is a way to think about the size-up stage and initial actions for any incident, which typically occur during the first 15 minutes after an incident is detected. See Figure 1-1, The Incident Lifecycle. These are general guidelines and can be tailored to fit your operation. See Figure 3-7 as a reference.

1. Detect the issue. This is usually a degradation of normal operating conditions, which initiates incident documentation.

2. Dispatch incident responders (varies by nature of issue detected).

3. Evaluate data provided by monitoring tools.

4. Assign level of severity (SEV) consistent with your company's terminology (more on this in "Triage" on page 54).

5. Establish incident communications (incident conference bridge, video conference, or text-based tools).

6. Ensure that the correct number and type of responders (SMEs, outside vendors, etc.) are dispatched, responding, and arriving on the incident conference bridge.

7. Establish command: IC identifies themselves by name as the IC and announces SEV to all incident responders.

8. IC provides an initial CAN report to responders engaged in the response. The timing of this will be determined by the IC based on the need to take action and the number of responders currently engaged. The report may be recorded in writing via group chat or other electronic tool used for incident documentation.

9. IC makes assignments to SMEs to investigate their technical domains (network, database, applications, etc.).

10. SMEs size up the incident and give CAN report to IC.

11. IC begins to formulate an incident action plan.

12. IC reassesses situation after initial 15 minutes (and on a regular basis as long as the incident is in progress). Additional actions to consider may include the following:

   — Assign operations personnel to manage continuing operations (ConOps).

   — Refine size-up and incident objectives if needed.

   — Estimate a reasonable mean time to repair (MTTR), which is important for determining the people and resources that may be needed beyond the initial IRT.

13. Notify appropriate customers, executives, and other interested parties as required, depending on the SEV level.

TRIAGE

A thorough size up will allow you to more accurately assign an appropriate SEV level, which will help you determine what kind of technical help (SMEs) is needed to resolve the incident. We often see organizations that have very granular rules to determine SEV levels, resulting in a large number of SEV or priority levels. We have also seen organizations waste valuable time on incidents trying to accurately determine the "right" SEV level from the many possible SEV levels available. We recommend a simple approach to SEV levels to streamline activities that need to occur during the first few minutes of any incident response. Figure 3-7 can be used as a template to think about potential SEV levels and frequency of occurrence in terms of color codes: Low Severity is a Green Box-issue; Moderate Severity is a Yellow-Box issue; High Severity is a Red-Box incident; and Disaster is a Black-Box incident.

Figure 3-7. Color-coded method classifies the severity (SEV) of a given incident

This approach can be useful to quickly align all responders to the significance of the incident. Green and yellow may be used to illustrate low levels of severity, such as users unable to log on to their corporate network or use an onsite printer. In general terms, if an incident has a well-defined set of solutions, and fixing it is more about executing a plan than finding the route toward a solution, the issue is probably a green- or yellow-box issue. In simple terms, this is a "see it, fix it" issue.

These are only examples of how SEV levels can be assigned and of course, each organization will have its own definition of SEV levels. We recommend that those definitions be broad enough so that every incident, on a relative basis, can be fit into one of the four color-coded boxes so that initial size up can be easily, clearly, and effectively communicated to all incident responders.

Note

It is important that the IC announces the SEV level to everyone involved in the response. This puts the incident in context so that all responders understand the urgency.

If the severity of the incident changes, the IC should announce the new SEV level. This helps maintain situational awareness for everyone assigned to the incident.

Think about the following situation, which is not at all related to incident response, to illustrate the point. Imagine walking out your front door and finding a flat tire on your car. The car is still there, it starts up just fine, and all the windows are intact—all good things. It seems as if the flat tire is the only thing wrong. You know that there are only a few solutions, all of them valid:

- Change the tire yourself

- Call a tow service

- Call a friend to help

You've encountered a finite, clear-cut, well-understood issue, and fixing it is more about choosing one of the apparent solutions rather than trying to solve an unknown issue. This is a classic "see it, fix it" issue, which would be triaged as *green-box issue* as seen in Figure 3-8.

Figure 3-8. Green-box issue. Solution is known; the resolution is more about executing a plan. Copyright: NejroN/www.123RF.com

If the severity were to escalate, for example, because the car wouldn't start, you'd be experiencing a *yellow-box issue.* The car is still there, which is good, and the windows are still intact and there is no evidence of significant damage, but the engine won't start. Much like a green-box issue, there is a limited pool of potential causes based on these symptoms. You might not know exactly what the issue is, but there is certainly more good news than bad, though you may have to seek the advice of an SME (mechanic) to solve it, as seen in Figure 3-9.

Figure 3-9. Yellow-box issue requiring SME involvement and diagnostics; copyright: kurhan / www.123RF.com

If the issue is novel, or so complicated or obscure that a solution requires trial and error, then you are transitioning to a *red-box incident.* These situations are complex and there may be no clear, easy path or set plan to follow to solve it. You may even have to resolve the incident in stages to get to a definitive fix. Using the car example, a red-box incident exists when you walk out your front door in the morning and the car is gone (Figure 3-10). Did you park your car in a tow-away zone or was it stolen? If it was stolen, think of all the things you have to sort out to bring the situation to resolution:

- Call the local police
- Notify your insurance company
- Find alternative ways to get to work

You may not know what kind of car you would choose to replace the missing one, whether the car might be recovered, or, if it is, what condition it will be in. There are lots of unknowns with red-box incidents and the outcome is uncertain.

Figure 3-10. Red-box incident: "I'm sure I parked my car right here."

Let's get back to incident response. Red-box incidents are where an IC *really* becomes valuable. As mentioned in Chapter 1, a good rule of thumb is this: as the SEV of the incident increases, so does the involvement and value of the IC. More significant incidents generally bring more responders, which typically requires stronger and more present leadership.

Note

Remember: high SEV incidents require strong leadership.

In short, *red-box incidents* are situations that are serious, may require many responders initially to form the IRT, and for which the response may go on for several hours or longer and expand the size of the IRT. There may be lot of trial and error and trailblazing to figure out an appropriate solution. The issue may be unique, with no clear cause or solution. These are the high-stakes events that could significantly damage the organization's finances and reputation, and erode trust with customers and confidence with investors.

Black-box incidents are disasters of a kind that may only happen once in the history of an organization. These are of a scale that could so adversely affect the organization that it may not recover from the financial impact or damage to reputation, trust, or confidence. Again, using the car example, a black-box incident would be a gasoline embargo or some catastrophic situation where gasoline is no longer commercially available. Black-box incidents may result in a "new normal" for the organization. See Figure 3-11.

*Figure 3-11. Black-box issue. A new normal emerges! Copyright: Setsiri Silapasuwanchai/www.
123rf.com*

Creating an organization-wide culture of incident response in which all responders speak a common language can be supported by using a color-coded system to assign SEV, perhaps along with specific written descriptions. This approach makes it easy for an IC to quickly refocus an off-track discussion in the following way:

> *Incident Commander: "Okay, I understand that we have a difference of opinion on how to solve this situation, but let's be reminded we are hard-down right now and working a serious red-box incident."*

ACT

The IC must eventually determine a course of action (*the incident action plan*) and pull the trigger on a plan (and *alternative plans*) to resolve the incident. There is no defined point in time where this should happen, but suffice it to say, the quicker the better. This sounds easier than it is, and a good plan includes at least the following components, some of which were developed in the size-up and triage phase:

- Engaged IC and appropriate SMEs
- A clear understanding of the issue, supported by data
- Input and support of trustworthy SMEs
- A straightforward objective or set of objectives for incident resolution
- Identification of the best- and worst-case scenarios of the proposed solution(s)
- A timeline for the incident resolution effort
- Continuous evaluation for progress and success
- A backup plan (or plans)

No matter what type of incident you are handling, there comes a time when planning is complete and action must be taken. Sometimes the transition from planning to action takes place quickly, especially when the solution is evident (such as in green- or yellow-box issues). In some cases, it takes time to develop a solid plan because the solution is not evident (like in red- or black-box incidents).

In most cases, the IC should take a moment to conduct a pre-action CAN report briefing to:

- Ensure that everyone on the incident conference bridge understands his/her role and mission.
- Confirm support from each appropriate stakeholder, which means literally that the IC asks each stakeholder to say out loud "I support the plan."
- Set expectations for desired outcomes. If the desired outcome is not achieved, the IC is the one who calls a hard stop to the action and/or directs the team to start on an alternate plan of attack.

The IC should get all relevant SMEs to affirmatively support the plan and verbalize that support on the bridge, or require the SME to provide a compelling reason for why it is not supported.

Incident Commander: "Okay, database says that we need to do a rolling restart on node 1 and it's going to take 15 minutes to see if that will clear our performance degradation. Database, do you support the plan?"_

> *Database:* "I support the plan."
>
> *Incident Commander:* "Network, do you support the plan?"
>
> *Network:* "I support the plan."
>
> *Incident Commander:* "Storage, do you support the plan?"
>
> *Storage:* "Well, I'm not too sure about this."
>
> *Incident Commander:* "Storage, what's your concern?"

This reinforces accountability of all SMEs and prevents second-guessing later, after the action is taken. The IC polls the SMEs one at a time and listens for strong and weak support for the plan, questioning further the SMEs who express weak support to expose any doubts about the ability of the plan to succeed. This is a critical phase of the incident. It's important for the IC to be an active listener for both the content of each SME's response and the tone, inflection, and emotion of each SME's response. If an SME says "I support the plan" in hushed tones rather than strongly, the IC should stop and ask a follow-up question (s) of that SME.

Note that there does not need to be 100% consensus. The IC must understand any objections and determine if they are strong enough to rethink the plan, but there is a big difference between a plan being "wrong" and it simply being "different" than someone else might have implemented in a similar situation. Additionally, it's common for ICs to ask if everyone agrees with a particular course of action rather than if there are any objections. Think about the group dynamic between the two. If the IC asks if there is agreement, the team members will feel compelled to answer with a yes or some other acknowledgment, and that takes time. If the IC only asks if there is disagreement with a particular plan, typically the time it takes to complete that task of polling the SMEs is far less. Remember, to shave hours off your MTTR, shave minutes off group discussions. To shave minutes off, shave seconds off each person-to-person conversation! Everyplace you can economize on communications is time you gain back for the incident response.

Information stewardship

Information is a commodity and everyone working the issue will have a unique hunger for it. To that end, the IC must ensure that all participants are stewards of information rather than owners of information. This means that anyone who knows anything about the issue and/or the possible solution(s) must offer that information to everyone on the event.

Information stewards freely share what they know for the greater good of the incident response. A key question for all incident responders is: "Who else needs to know what I know?" Any single piece of information can be used in any number of ways by any number of people or the functions they represent. The key to good information management is to provide relevant facts and keep opinions and/or speculation in check unless asked.

A few key concepts will help the IC stay focused and not get overwhelmed by information and the management of that information:

- There is no good or bad news—just news.
- Data is nothing more than raw facts.
- Once put into context, data can be turned into actionable information.
- Information is not the same as opinion; keep the two separate.
- Solve first, then notify those that need to be notified when appropriate.
- Be concise.
- Ask one question; get one answer.
- Summarize often, even if you don't think you need to. This ensures consistent understanding among all participants.
- If you can't quickly explain what you are doing, maybe you aren't clear in your own mind.
- Accept the facts as they are and don't try to spin the situation into something it is not.
- Hope is a poor planning tool.

- Don't over-report or under-report anything.

REVIEW

There are two aspects to the Review part of STAR for the IC: 1) periodically review the incident response while it is on-going; and 2) set defined operational periods to summarize current conditions, benchmark progress, and report to external stakeholders. As the incident progresses in time, the IC must continually review and assess how the incident response is going and move the incident resolution forward. The IC can use the CAN report to redirect the discussion and refocus resolution efforts as needed. Each CAN report is a good time for the IC to ask; "Should we bring anyone else onto this bridge?" It's the IC's responsibility to determine if more of the same or different resources (SMEs, external vendors, etc.) are needed at any point in the incident response.

For incidents of longer time duration, the IC may formalize the review process.

The *operational period* is a defined period of time that identifies a cadence or frequency for specific actions to be taken and is set by the IC. For example, the IC could initially establish informational briefings (using the CAN report format) at the 30-minute mark, and then every 30-minutes, unless the IC determines that they can be held less frequently. Operational briefings are useful as they create a defined time frame and set of behavioral objectives that are outlined for the entire group of incident responders.

Toward the end of the incident, a key to incident resolution is to clearly identify what a successful solution will look like (i.e., the desired end state). The final stages of many incidents are often ambiguous or poorly defined. It may not be clear that the solution is definitive and that a return to a normal state of operations (peacetime) is certain. Whatever the final incident resolution is, the IC must clearly communicate to the IRT and other stakeholders that the incident has been resolved. The IC should then release resources so they can return to other duties in the organization.

The IC must determine if the end state of the incident results in a return to pre-event conditions or some adaptive state. For example, a piece of code may be written to temporarily get the system restored but not address the underlying issue. The long-term ramifications of a short-term fix like this might not be immediately understood. A fix now could result in planting a time bomb that might show up later. Chances are that the temporary fix will not be documented and future incidents could eventually become more complicated.

Either case might be an acceptable return to peacetime, but if a new normal is put in place, it is vital to the team to perform two comprehensive reviews. First, an *After Action Review* (AAR) should be conducted to constructively evaluate the people and their response to the incident in order to identify lessons learned and improve future responses. Second, a *Root Cause Analysis* (RCA), or whatever term you use, should be conducted by the technical team to determine the root cause(s) and reason(s) to determine why the technology failed. RCAs are best done after the incident, not during! Simply stated, RCAs are to figure out what broke and AARs are to figure out how the people responded to the thing(s) that broke.

It is critical to communicate the AAR and RCA information to the peacetime organization so the terms of the adaptive change are documented and understood. All organizations, when faced with an incident situation—some significant disturbance in the operating environment—will respond with accepting the change, rejecting the change, or adapting in some way to the change. The IC will be responsible for the change, and must ensure that the incident is used as a learning opportunity and not just viewed as a lucky near miss!

Figure 3-12 brings it all together in a flowchart.

IMS/IC FLowchart

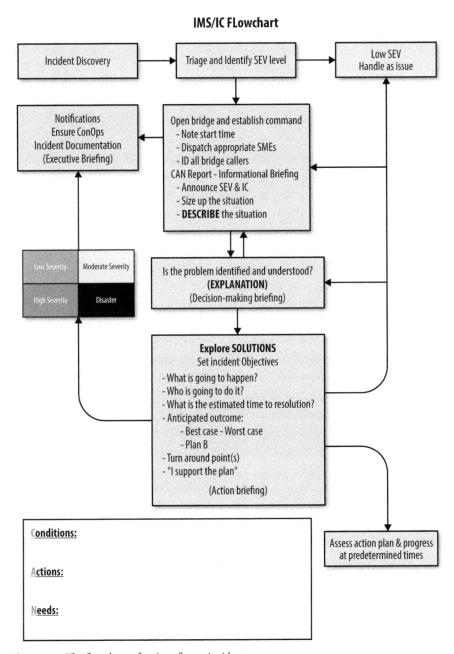

Figure 3-12. The flowchart of actions for an incident

It's All About TIME

As mentioned in Chapter 1, uptime and downtime are broad representations of two operational states for a company that delivers service or is engaged in any kind of operations. Incident response is absolutely a time-sensitive activity, and for every second, minute, or hour(s) a company is impacted, a clock is running that increases financial and reputational risk and erodes trust and confidence.

What's a minute worth to your company? It will vary by company, but certainly it would include these metrics: company revenue, company earnings, company stock price, contractual penalties for missing service level agreements (SLAs) with customer(s); credits on current billing for lost uptime; future credits for lost uptime; insurance claims; legal costs; lost sales opportunities with current customers and prospective customers; aggressive response by competitor(s); reporting to regulatory agencies; costs for public relations and advertising campaigns. For example, a simple calculation is to take the company's most recent reported revenue (multiply by 12 if monthly or by 4 if quarterly) and divide by 525,600 (minutes in a calendar year). Arguably, companies run multiple systems and revenue may come from many sources besides the system in downtime, but it's an attempt to quantify downtime in financial terms. One online retailer includes lost sales in every AAR and RCA, to correlate the technical issue with business impact. If you have data from past incidents to estimate what a minute is worth in your company, by all means collect it! It may be hard to calculate depending on your business, but it will likely be a sobering number that underscores the need to resolve incidents quickly and efficiently. As you can see, an incident is detected as a technical issue but the IC and IRT are in reality resolving a business issue.

To that end, the IC is to some degree the time keeper of the incident and is responsible for keeping incidents moving forward with purpose. As we have discussed previously, the IC makes assignments by function to SME resources, with time deadlines, and then must hold those SMEs accountable to time. To help you remember the importance of time, we've developed an acronym that may help an IC stay focused on four important time-influencing aspects of leading an incident response. TIME, which stands for: *tone, interaction, management,* and *engagement.*

TONE

A critical part of incident leadership is ensuring that everyone participating in the response shares a sense of urgency, purpose, and direction. The IC, as the leader of this high-speed collaboration, must demonstrate good command presence and set the *tone*, which is the general demeanor and attitude of the incident responders participating in the resolution effort.

Think back to well-run incidents you may have been part of and give some thought to the leadership. You certainly know when you are following a person who displays confidence and poise and inspires the followers, and you know equally well when you are following a leader who does none of those things. It's easy to spot a leader who is overbearing, has weak presence, or is indecisive.

Incident response can be a mentally taxing, stressful, frustrating, rewarding, and an awesome experience all during the same response. It is up to the IC to identify unwanted distractions and disruptions to the incident response environment. Whether those distractions or disruptions result from poor interactions or attitudes between incident responders, ineffective communications, or perhaps not having the right technical expertise working the issue, it is up to the Incident Commander to correct the issue(s).

Note

Here's an easy way to think of the role of the IC in setting the tone of the incident: As the IC's tone goes, so goes the responder's tone.

If the incident is being managed over a conference call bridge, the IC should speak with confidence and authority (i.e., how things are said) and ensure that the interactions between the incident responders are respectful, clear, specific, and accurate (i.e., what is said). It's very common for responders to mimic the tone set by the IC. For example, if the IC has a confrontational tone, so may the incident responders. If the IC is supportive and respectful, the responders typically follow suit.

This is certainly not a hard-and-fast rule, and there are so many factors that influence human behavior that it's hard to make any absolute statements, but here's the key takeaway: *the IC should be conscious of the need to create and maintain a positive and directed work environment, regardless of the method of communication*. Setting the tone is the basic building block upon which clarity and direction are built. Figure 3-13 lays out a way to think about why the behavior and position of the IC is such an important link in the chain of getting everyone on the same page.

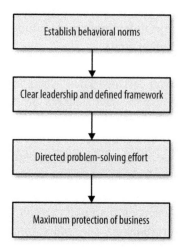

Figure 3-13. Incident management is about clarity, alignment, and attitude—getting the right people to the right place at the right time to make the right decisions!

Note

Specific: clearly defined
Accurate: representing the truth

INTERACTION

As part of the overall tone of the incident, the way in which the incident respond-ers interact is important. Unproductive or wandering conversations waste time. Confrontational or antagonistic behavior can degrade the morale of the respond-ers. To that end, the IC must be mindful of two important things:

- Are incident responders participating to their fullest technical capabilities?

- Are incident responders interacting with each other respectfully, truth-fully, ego-free, and with the goal of resolving the incident as a team in the shortest amount of time possible?

It's key that the IC actively listens to the discussions among the responders and moderates accordingly. Disagreements may arise during the discussions and that is absolutely acceptable. In fact, disagreements may even lead to better or different conclusions or a new course of action, as long as the discussions remain directed, productive, nonconfrontational, and focused on the topic. This may sound simple and straightforward, and in most cases it is, but every IC should pay close attention to how the incident responders are conducting themselves during the response.

Responder personality types

We've identified a list of common personalities you may interact with during an incident response. These personalities are described in a broad sense and a bit tongue in cheek to make it more interesting. Much like the fire service, the IT world is filled with talented, opinionated, and sometimes outspoken people who must work together during an incident, put their superpowers to use, and resolve the incident in the shortest time possible.

Note

Managing the variety of personalities that arrive to resolve the incident can be as challenging as the incident itself!

These 14 personalities are offered only to serve only as a reminder that when an incident conference call bridge or other form of incident communication is opened, the "game is on" to resolve the incident. The IC is in charge of the people-to-people aspect of the incident and these personalities play a part in the success or failure of the incident resolution effort.

We aren't psychologists and these personalities are not based in hard or soft science. They are based on people we have run across in our incident response career. Keep in mind that just because the right job functions respond to the incident, that doesn't mean that all of the people will play nice together!

An IC must quickly identify circumstances where the technical talent may not be interacting effectively and identify what may be preventing the group from working together smoothly. Examples may include two engineers arguing over a particular course of action or reason for the technology failure rather than staying focused on finding the best solution. Engineers love to be engineers and build or fix things, and they typically also like to be right! The conversation may have strayed off the path of a best course of action and become more of an "I'm smarter than you and let me tell you all the reasons why" interaction. We've heard these conversations on recorded incident conference bridges and can say for certain they are distracting and debilitating to the overall effort and must be dealt with quickly by the IC. There is a difference between a long productive discussion and one that becomes a struggle for intellectual superiority.

Another example may be an SME who arrives on the call with a "Why am I here?" or "I have much better things to do with my time" attitude. This likely occurred due to a PROCESS failure outlined in Chapter 1 where the person is simply unaware of their role in the incident response. The IC now has a personality issue to handle in order to keep the effort on track, on top of the main goal of resolving the incident in the shortest time possible. Add other situational challenges typically encountered on incident conference call bridges such as loud background noise, kids yelling and dogs barking, language barriers, executives, or other senior persons swooping in and taking over an incident response, or just simply having a group that lacks a sense of urgency in the response. Adding these situational challenges to the myriad personalities that may be involved and the IC has a recipe for awesomeness or difficulty or something in between.

In any case, these situational examples are all populated with people who bring with them their own set of personality traits, biases, daily or hourly attitudes, and everything else that goes into human behavior. So read on, and see if some of the personalities we identify exist in your orbit of incident response and how you might handle them as an IC during the incident. These are not indictments of any one person or persona, just observations and food for thought.

Of course, after the incident has been resolved, the IC has choices to mitigate unproductive behaviors in the future. First, the IC can and should make these observations part of the AAR, but in a positive and constructive way. If other incident responders saw the same offending behaviors and the IC doesn't address it during the AAR, it undermines the authority and integrity of the IC and reinforces the individual displaying the offending behavior. Second, the IC can have an offline conversation with the offending incident responder or their manager in order to point out and correct the behaviors. These conversations should stay positive and focused on correcting the behavior and not attacking the individual. The IC must create a safe, collaborative, and productive environment for future incidents because of the risk to the company's finances and reputation and erosion of trust and confidence.

The Awesome Contributor This first personality sets the gold standard for an SME or anyone else who joins the incident response. They are easy to get along with, helpful and pleasant, and know their job. We'll call them the *Awesome Contributor*, or AC. Every IC wants a team full of ACs!

- Arrives in a timely fashion and with a sense of urgency.
- Leaves ego and attitudes at the door.
- Announces themselves by name and by function.
- Is operationally ready to contribute (computer, network, access to monitoring/diagnostic tools, etc.).
- Is technically proficient in the functional domain.
- Is available for the duration of the incident.
- If operating on an incident bridge, ensures that work environment is quiet.
- Speaks up and speaks clearly.
- Provides specific, direct, and factual answers to questions.
- Interacts effectively with others.
- Respects the IC's timeline for completing assigned tasks.
- Will request more help if necessary.
- Stays focused on the event.

The Quiet One

- May be uncomfortable speaking up in a group.
- Little interaction on an incident conference bridge unless called out by name specifically or a natural pathway is created for their contribution.
- May be reserved in speech and actions but can provide invaluable insights and information.

Incident Commander Tactics:

- Don't ignore or discount the Quiet One as uninterested or unqualified based on the amount of interaction.
- Ask direct questions of the Quiet One by name/function to create an entry point for them to participate in the conversation.

- If Quiet Ones are being rolled over in the discussion, take action to give them airtime!

The Naysayer

- Typically outspoken, with a large, loud personality.

- Frequently comes across as negative.

- Often cites past history as justification why a current idea or plan won't work.

- May be a dissenting opinion simply for the sake of dissension.

- Finds many reasons why something won't work but few reasons why it will.

- Often "what ifs" all plans or ideas to the extreme.

- May be entrenched in their own position and defend it at all costs.

Incident Commander Tactics:

- The Naysayer isn't always wrong, so beware of discounting the issues they raise just because they may be difficult to deal with during the incident.

- Require specificity when Naysayers throw up obstacles or dissension.

- Ask the Naysayer for data that supports their position.

- Don't engage in verbal sparring.

The IC may need to tell a Naysayer they are in a minority opinion on a topic or idea and that the incident response must move forward. Remember that consensus is not always possible on every action taken during a response.

The Overbearing One

- Frequently identified in the peacetime organization as a "know-it-all."
- Like the Naysayer, overbearing people typically have large, loud personalities.
- Puts people on the defensive.
- Can't or won't see other perspectives.
- Can't seem to be agreeable without some caveat or reason.
- May be a person that commonly likes to push buttons and/or push limits of other people.
- May be impulsive.
- Quick to pass judgment and make snap decisions.
- May not easily accept being wrong or that others are making contributions that appear to be more useful.

Incident Commander Tactics:

- Stay calm and don't engage in verbal or written sparring.
- Beware of very opinionated suggestions that may be more colorful and grandiose than helpful.
- Use other incident response participants to help evaluate the ideas offered by the Overbearing One.
- Avoid pointing out directly that the Overbearing One is wrong.
- May be useful to assign tasks to an Overbearing One that take them off the main communications channel. Make the assignment technically challenging and not busy work. Indicate its importance to the incident response.

The Over Explainer

- Intelligent, competent, confident, and talented.

- Gives lengthy explanations whenever a question is asked (tells you how watches are made when you ask what time it is).

- Believes they are being helpful.

- Generally doesn't provide "yes" or "no" answers.

- Adds personal stories or historical background to descriptions or explanations that may or may not be relevant.

- Not overtly disruptive but may steal time away with needless detail.

- Provides explanations when asked for solutions.

- Wants to make sure everybody knows how the technology works.

Incident Commander Tactics:

- Recognize the Over Explainer and keep them in check. Interrupt if necessary once the required information is obtained.

- Many Over Explainers don't recognize the behavior pattern in themselves.

- Beware when two Over Explainers are engaged. They may take you on a detailed journey of discussion that may or may not be useful and consume unrecoverable time!

- Give them a timeline prior to asking a question. An example might go something like this, "Mary, it sounds like we need to get an opinion on this message queue lag, can you explain that to me in a minute or less?"

The Joker

- Constantly injecting humor or irrelevant comments into the conversation, just like a class clown.

- Doesn't make the switch from peacetime to wartime.

- Creates an environment that gives others permission to join and escalate.

- Can prevent the entire incident response from making the switch from peacetime to wartime.
- Typically loves attention.
- May have or bring followers to the incident response.
- Believes they are funny.
- Most have high self-esteem and are usually good resolvers.
- Doesn't take the urgency or gravity of the incident seriously.

Incident Commander Tactics:

- Limit the Joker's opportunities to disrupt early in the incident. If left unchecked, it could be difficult to reign in.
- If behavior persists, be direct in reminding the Joker to stay focused.
- While this personality may not seem toxic to an incident response effort, be careful not to indulge the Joker or encourage the behavior.
- Remind the Joker of the urgency and gravity of the incident to the business.

The Uncertain Contributor

- May be hard to pin down when looking for specific information or recommendations.
- Frequently needs more time to "check one more thing" before taking action.
- The higher the stakes, the higher the level of uncertainty.
- Frequently uses hedging or uncertain language when offering opinions or recommendations. You might hear words like "well," "maybe," "perhaps," "it could be," or "it might."
- The Uncertain Contributor may try to find "the perfect solution" or 100% certainty even when it's not possible or practical to do so.

Incident Commander Tactics:

- Demand specificity and accuracy.

- Don't let the perfect be the enemy of the good.

- Phrase questions to the Uncertain Contributor that only require yes or no answers.

- If Uncertain Contributor won't answer yes or no questions, re-phrase question into a range of certainty. For example, "On a scale of 1 to 10, with 10 being the most certain, what's the number you'd assign your recommendation?"

- With this personality (and the others for that matter), ask one question and get one answer. Avoid long or complicated questions that allow the Uncertain Contributor to pick and choose what part of the question to answer. Think specifically about what information you want and ask questions as simply and directly as possible.

- Involve other SMEs to bolster, corroborate, or even refute their opinions and recommendations of the Uncertain Contributor.

- Be prepared to get another SME from the same domain to replace or assist the Uncertain Contributor.

The Gunslinger

- The Gunslinger is talented, very knowledgeable, and extremely valuable to the organization, and the Gunslinger *knows it!*

- The Gunslinger likely has deep technical knowledge in a mission-critical, peacetime activity.

- The Gunslinger may have an eclectic personality and doesn't collaborate well with others, but that behavior is tolerated (and therefore reinforced) by the company because they are so good at what they do and are indispensable to the organization.

- The company may reinforce the Gunslinger's peacetime value and role in wartime incidents.

- The Gunslinger is often called specifically because he or she has built a reputation as a key problem-solver and "go to" person.

- Will drop names, jargon, and obscure facts to solidify their position.

- Likes to represent that they have all the technical, historical, and institutional knowledge about any issue.

- The Gunslinger will have the deepest technical knowledge, is often right, and will intimidate anyone who crosses their path.

- Many won't cross their path.

- Likely will have a large, loud, and supremely confident personality.

- May have the attitude "This is a huge issue and mere mortals cannot understand it, so that's why you called me. I'm the only person who can fix this. I am here now to save the day and then I will go and solve another giant issue. Stand back."

- Doesn't tolerate competition well.

- Won't want to stay past taking the big actions.

- Doesn't like administration and documenting actions.

Incident Commander Tactics:

- Don't confuse the confidence of the Gunslinger with his or her ability to get to the right answer.

- Take steps to prevent the Gunslinger from informally assuming the role of IC and taking over the incident response effort.

- As with the Uncertain Contributor, it may be wise to structure questions in such a way as to not provide a stage for the Gunslinger to take over the incident response effort.

- Don't engage technically one on one with the Gunslinger.

- Reinforce often the IC's role by name and SEV of the incident.

- Keep the relationship between the IC and Gunslinger at the "resolve the incident in the shortest amount of time" level.

- Appeal to their Gunslinger persona. Use language like "I really need your help here. We're hard down and you know this system inside and out."

- This personality is challenging in that it may be difficult to distinguish a key person with unique knowledge, skill, or talent from the Gunslinger personality. Gunslingers may be more intimidating than helpful.

- Once right does not mean always right!

The Interrupter

- Bursts into the middle of conversations without permission.

- May have been lurking on an incident conference bridge or other communications channel prior to interrupting.

- Routinely cuts off others during conversation.

- Believes they have critical information to add to any conversation.

- Continuously seeks attention.

- Others may interrupt sensing implicit permission from the Incident Commander to do so.

- Interrupters typically aren't good listeners.

- They only want to talk rather than carrying on a two-way conversation.

Incident Commander Tactics:

- Keep the Interrupter in check by observing and remarking on the behavior early.

- Interrupters can usually be kept in check by ignoring them and commenting directly to the people whose conversation they are interrupting.

- Ask Interrupters to wait for their turn to enter the discussion.

- The IC needs to be firm and assertive with the Interrupter, because the meek IC will get rolled over by the Interrupter.

- Reinforce often the IC's role by name and SEV of the incident.

The Grenade Thrower

- May derail a plan or line of thinking after decisions have been made.

- Creates fear, uncertainty, and doubt.

- Diverts attention from the main points or plan with "what ifs" to the point that nothing looks like a good idea.

- Uses the language of uncertainty, including "have you thought of that?" or "that might happen."

- This personality is difficult to recognize because raising objections and "what if" points are healthy when done at the right time and for the right reasons.

- May not recognize this tendency in themselves and doesn't see the behavior as distracting.

Incident Commander Tactics:

- If it appears that the Grenade Thrower has lobbed a distraction, refocus the discussion with a CAN report and stick to the verifiable facts. Facts are kryptonite to the Grenade Thrower.

- Grenade Throwers often cite the possibility of an extreme positive or negative outcome as justification for actions. The IC should acknowledge all possibilities, but keep the group focused on probabilities. Possible outcomes can be initially measured by yes or no.

- Ask questions focused on probabilities of occurrence right now and within numerical ranges. For example, is it possible that an asteroid will crash in to the earth and cause massive damage? The answer is yes, of course, because it's wrong to say it's impossible. It has happened before and even though it's been millennia since the event, it did happen and is therefore possible, although the probabilities are minimal. Ask the question this way, "On a scale of 0 to 100%, what's the probability that an asteroid will crash to the earth today and cause massive damage?" Be careful to cut off any answer that goes down a rabbit hole of technical definitions, like if the Grenade Thrower replies "well, what's massive damage?"

- If the answer is no to a possibility question, then the issue is solved right there. For example, is it possible to walk across the ocean? The answer is no, which makes any further discussion of the event irrelevant and nothing more than an interesting thought experiment at best. In this context, the word "probable" may be interchanged with the word "likely," indicating a strong sense that the event or consequence may occur.

- An event may be possible but unlikely, which is where the Grenade Thrower may base an opinion, argument, or justification. If needed, an IC can help defeat the Grenade Thrower by distinguishing between possible and likely/probable when sorting through options or dissension on a course of action. An IC may poll the incident response group and ask if a particular outcome to an action is possible or likely/probable. Anything possible becomes some degree of likely. The groups can then rank the likely events on a 1 to 10 scale with 1 being least likely and 10 being most likely.

The Chicken Little

- Like Chicken Little, behaves like "the sky is falling, the sky is falling!"
- Views every incident as a catastrophe.
- Tends to focus on worst-case-scenario viewpoints.
- "If we don't fix this, the data center will melt into the ground, the company will go bankrupt, and we'll all be out of a job."
- Creates unhealthy sense of urgency among responders.
- Typically thinks conservatively when it comes to taking action.

Incident Commander Tactics:

- Keep responders focused on efforts being taken to resolve the incident.
- Summarize regularly with CAN reports.
- Focus on facts and known conditions.

- Refer to the probable versus likely thinking outlined in the Grenade Thrower personality in order to keep a sense of reality.
- Avoid letting the Chicken Little take the incident response off course.

The Lurker

- Calls into the incident conference call bridge or other communications channel and then doesn't identify himself.
- Doesn't answer when roll call is being taken.
- Stays silent in the shadows and goes undetected by the IC and other incident responders.
- Won't participate until they believe it is necessary and then chimes in without warning.
- May drop off a bridge and never identify themselves.
- Likely behaves as a serial Lurker on multiple incident conference bridges over long periods of time.
- Might be a high-ranking peacetime resource or executive who "just wants to hear what's going on."

Incident Commander Tactics:

- Acknowledge and ensure that every incident responder is identified when arriving to participate.
- On longer incidents, conduct a *Personnel Accountability Report* (PAR) to identify all persons on the incident. PAR is based on the initial roll call and keeps track of whether incident responders are still on the incident conference bridge.
- Maintain operational security (OpSec) on the incident conference bridge. Confirm that whoever has access to the incident communications channel *should* have access to the communications channel. For example, what would be the impact to your company if customers or the press entered the incident conference call bridge during a high SEV incident?

- The IC will never know who may be listening unless you take steps to find out.

- It's okay for persons to join the incident conference call bridge and stand by without contributing as long as the IC knows who is on the bridge.

- The IC should always know the roster of resources available to be engaged in the incident response.

The Jumper (to Conclusions)

- Quick to arrive at a conclusion without fully investigating a situation, idea, thought, etc.

- Generally uses intuition, pattern recognition, past experience, or "rules of thumb."

- The Jumper may be right or wrong, but one thing is for sure—they jump quick!

- Likes others to think of them as smart because they can process information faster than anybody else.

- High tolerance for risk.

- Believes SEV of incident warrants quick decisions.

- The Jumper may be very experienced and relies on that body of experience to make quick decisions.

- Again, the Jumper may often be right based on inference (something believed to be true based on previous experience).

Incident Commander Tactics:

- Ensure that all incident responders are clear when discussing facts (able to be proven true or false) or opinions (something not measured against an objective standard).

- Keep the Jumper (and everyone else for that matter) focused on fact-based decision-making.

- The IC should always be evaluating information and placing it in the fact, inference, or opinion category to weight it correctly in the decision-making process.

- Question the Jumper to produce evidence of their position.

- Remind the incident responders that the goal of incident response decision-making is to make the best decision in the shortest amount of time, not to just make quick decisions.

The Tunnel Rat

- Typically takes a very narrow point of view or has focus on a single priority (tunnel vision).

- Difficult to move them off their position even in the face of compelling evidence.

- Will strongly defend position against other people.

- May question other people's qualifications to discredit them.

- Uses strong language of conviction, like "absolutely," "we must," and "can't you see it?"

- May exhibit confirmation bias (take in, use, or interpret only the information that favorably supports his or her positon, belief, etc.).

- May ignore or downplay information that does not support their position.

Incident Commander Tactics:

- Don't engage in a circular discussion with the Tunnel Rat.

- Tunnel Rat may only find new or different information to support their position.

- IC may agree to disagree on a particular point and move on.

- Be factual in briefings.

- Prevent the Tunnel Rat from speculating or forming opinions that cannot be verified.

Again, we are not professional psychologists and these personalities are not offered as character assassinations or intended to be derogatory in any way. These are simply our observation of behaviors over long careers in incident response. It's also a reminder that there are a lot of big, opinionated personalities in the IT field. If you are an IC and you recognize that one (or more) of these personalities (or the many more that exist) are present and adversely impacting the incident response effort, be assertive to maintain or restore a positive and directed tone to the response!

MANAGEMENT

Figure 3-14 illustrates a comparison between situational issues that may occur on the incident conference bridge in conjunction with the personalities that may be in play.

Situations	Personalities
- Long unproductive conversations	- The Awesome Contributor
- Bad SME	- The Naysayer
- Team friction	- The Over Explainer
- Background noise	- The Uncertain Contributor
- Language challenges	- The Gunslinger
- Cultural challenges	- The Interrupter
- Lack of progress	- The Grenade Thrower
- Lack of sense of urgency	- Chicken Little
- Fatigue	- The Lurker
- Pressure from executives	- The Tunnel Rat

Figure 3-14. Situational issues that may occur on the incident conference bridge in conjunction with the personalities that may be in play

The column on the left are time-stealing situations that may sap energy and focus from the incident response, especially when encountered on an incident conference bridge. To some degree, these situations represent the "things" of people management. The column on the right lists some of the personalities that may be participating in the incident response. To that end, an IC must be mindful of both columns and the interplay between them on a moment-by-moment basis.

It could be possible that an IC has a small group of incident responders with an Awesome Contributor, an Uncertain Contributor, and a Joker, all having an unproductive discussion and wasting time. It is also possible to have a team entirely made up of Awesome Contributors yet still not be efficiently operating if there is interpersonal friction between them, they begin to tire, or perhaps they lack a sense of urgency to resolve the incident. Literally, the combination of situations and personalities can change from incident to incident, an perhaps even within the same incident.

So you see, it is delicate balancing act for an IC to make a distinction between the personalities operating on the incident and the situational issues that may also be in play. There is no perfect recipe for success, but it is possible to at least recognize them when they occur and take mindful action to try to unwind whatever is complicating the incident response effort.

ENGAGEMENT

Engagement is in the last part of the TIME mnemonic. It serves as an important reminder that an IC must ensure that the right people are engaged in the incident resolution effort and that if more or different resources (SMEs, vendors, etc.) are needed, they should be called to participate quickly. Engagement is about two main parts for incident responders: dispatch and state.

The first part of engagement is the way in which people are called upon to respond. In IT, the word "notification" is used as the way to notify people. Many people may be notified when an alert occurs via a number of different notification tools. They may be notified for a wide variety of reasons: to fix the issue; to determine the customer impact of the issue; to craft communications to stakeholders about the issue; to escalate the issue if needed; to inform the executives of the issue. We've seen many companies notify a large number of people, who then join the incident conference bridge and assemble into a large, unwieldy, leaderless group. The incident conference call bridge turns into a free-for-all where dominant personalities rule until the incident is resolved. We have not encountered a single person or company that views that scenario as productive!

We believe a definition of terms is needed in IT. The word "notify" in this context means "to inform a person of information that they should know." There is NOT an explicit call to action in the word "notify." The word "dispatch" in this context means "to inform a person of information that they should know and that requires them to take action." There is an explicit call to action in the word "dispatch." In IT, there is an implicit call to action in the word "notify," which is why a large number of people who are notified join incident conference bridges.

In the fire service, dispatch is a specialized function that resides in the 911 call center. When a 911 call is received by a 911 call center, the 911 call taker asks questions of the 911 caller and generates an alert (much like a monitoring tool generates an alert). The 911 call taker transmits information about the 911 call (address, nature of emergency, etc.) to the dispatcher who performs a dispatch function to the appropriate fire resources based on address and incident response needed. This is not a notify function. Using the preceding definitions, to "notify" the fire engine at Station 1 is not an explicit call to action. Of course, if your home were on fire, you would prefer dispatch to notify!

As a fire resource, being dispatched is not a request to respond or the option to respond—it's a directive. If a fire engine or a firefighter is on-call, that resource is identified in the incident response matrix as available to respond: trained, equipped, and prepared to perform the expected function; will respond within the expected time frame and will remain engaged in the incident response until released by the IC. In short, it's an agreement between the incident responder and the dispatch function that guarantees an incident response. Whatever the issue, time of day, or conflict that may exist between responding and/or other nonincident job requirements, the incident responder will fulfill, to the best of her ability, all the expectations that come with being *available* to participate in the response. Dispatch of incident resources is important because that identifies the IC's workforce, which is a critical element in completing a proper size-up.

The second part of engagement is the state of an incident response resource. The IRT in a company is analogous to the fire department, except it responds to IT incidents. As the IT "fire department" within a company, the incident responders are really no different. To that end, when IT responders are on call, they always exist in only one of seven states of being:

1. Available to respond.

2. Dispatched.

3. Responding (transitioning from available, a peacetime activity, to attached to the incident, a wartime activity).

4. On scene (identified as arrived and present on an incident conference call bridge or other communications channel).

5. Assigned a task by the IC.

6. Staged (not currently assigned a task by the Incident Commander). Staged is a state, which is still an active participant in the incident response even though not directly involved. Staged is not lurking because the incident responder is identified, but perhaps not directly involved in the resolution activities. The IC doesn't want to release the incident responder from the pool of resources just yet but wants the incident responder to be ready for an assigned task on the incident conference bridge at a moment's notice.

7. Released back to available status.

Again, the base state of any incident responder in peacetime is *available*. From there, the incident responder can transition back and forth among the other states as required by the incident needs and directed by the IC. The first four states are where valuable time can be saved or lost. These are the only areas in the Incident Lifecycle that a company can control and they make up the MTTA. Ineffective dispatch procedures, ambiguity about resources that should be available, and poor notification technology are common places in the Incident Lifecycle where time is lost. We've heard time after time from companies large and small that it's common to need a particular SME and contact them, only to have them arrive and wonder why they've been asked to join the response.

These and other woes can be cured when PROCESS is used as a planning tool to ensure that dispatching the talent is predictable, repeatable, and clear. This includes requesting incident resources beyond the original dispatch, when more or different technical expertise is needed. Every company that performs incident operations should have very clear expectations about how to get the right people together to resolve the incident in the shortest amount of time.

On that note, we'd again like to mention that more is not always better when it comes to human resources. If you've participated in a spray-and-pray incident response process, you will likely agree that it's not the most effective way to do business.

Automated notification systems are great tools to speed up dispatching your responders, but we offer this caution: beware of simply mapping notification dysfunction into a notification tool. It's just a quicker way to get the wrong incident responders! Some companies map their dispatch of incident responders to SEV levels and the most common SME functions required for most incidents. However it's done, we recommend an evaluated and directed way to identify and dispatch the right SMEs because it can save substantial amounts of time in incident response.

Additionally, a word is needed on something called reflex time. *Reflex time* is the amount of time that elapses between the moment you realize a need for a resource and the moment that resource arrives. Every IC should consider reflex time when it comes to obtaining initial talent or calling for more or different resources. There's an old adage in the fire service that goes like this: "If you think you need it, call for it early" because it takes time for the "it" to arrive. If you think you need something or someone to help fix something, get it sooner rather than later. Better to have an incident resource dispatched, responding, on scene, or staged than trying to track down when you need it. If the IC no longer needs an incident responder, release it.

There is a fear of alert fatigue if incident resources are often called and not needed. There is no perfectly defined trigger point for calling or not calling for whatever you need. But think back to the seven states of being and when an incident responder is *available*, it means he or she is *available*. That's it. They are not available only when the SEV is high or when their involvement is guaranteed. They are available, period.

Again, the fire department offers a good example here. Firefighters respond frequently to false alarms or incidents that prove to be less severe than initially reported, but that is part of the job and inevitable in the incident response business. However, only after an issue was detected, reported, dispatched and investigated by the fire department was it then deemed a "false alarm." To be clear, it's annoying at times, but it's the job that comes with accepting the duties of incident response. This is why formally evaluating the incident response, as well as how the IC led and managed the incident and the IRT responded, is so crucial. It provides opportunities to look back at all facets of the incident resolution effort and make adjustments to the entire incident response mechanism.

Keep in mind that incident response is a constantly evolving activity within an organization. It is seldom the case that a company is perfect in the way it handles incidents and it has the luxury of locking down the way in which it responds into a perfectly synchronized and well-oiled machine. The IT environment is constantly scaling, changing, and becoming more complex. People will come and go on the IRT and companies expand or change services. One thing that is true about operations is this: if you have operations, you will have incident operations and it will be a moving target over time to find perfection!

Summary

Things are managed and people are led. An incident is a thing to be managed and the Incident Management System (IMS) is the best practice management framework. The incident responders are the people to be led and the IC is the best practice leadership role. Incident management is a team sport of many different kinds of people from ICs to SMEs to executives. Understanding how to get the best performance out of the incident responders is a key responsibility of the IC.

- The IC's job is to bring order and direction to the chaotic nature of an incident.
- The IC is responsible for the overall management of the incident.
- ICs must set incident objectives and priorities on every incident.
- It is the IC's responsibility to drive the incident forward toward resolution in the shortest amount of time possible.
- ICs must delegate tasks and supervision when necessary.
- Use the CAN report (conditions, actions, needs) for briefings.
- Use the STAR acronym (size up, triage, act, review) to remember the important elements of incident response.
- Incident response is a person-to-person activity, and being mindful of the human interaction is vital.
- An IC should consider the elements listed in TIME as a guide for tone, interaction, management, and engagement during an incident response.
- The IC should be aware of the personalities and situations involved in the response and ensure that all interpersonal interactions are positive and beneficial to the resolution effort.
- There is a marked difference between dispatch and notification of incident responders.

4

Scaling the Incident Response

Incident Response and Escalation

Small incidents with low impact typically require less people and management framework, and perhaps rely more on problem solving by individuals. Large problems with high impact typically require more incident responders, more management framework, more teamwork, more tasks to complete and track, more stress, and more business impact to consider. These larger incidents generally require a robust management framework to stay organized and a stronger Incident Commander to keep the effort moving forward in a clear and purposeful manner.

There is no perfect management formula for either situation and no hard-and-fast rules. It's up to each Incident Commander to create the right mixture of command and framework to create the most effective incident resolution environment, which is matched to the size and scope of the incident. Part of being a good Incident Commander is the ability to know how to expertly mix the elements of command, framework, and problem-solving.

In some cases, it may appear unnecessary to adhere to a formal command structure on what seems like a minor issue (green- or yellow-box issue), but think of it this way: each incident response reinforces the use of the process for all incident responders because skill and proficiency are mastered by repetition.

If IMS is only activated for large incidents (red- or black-box incidents), those skills and proficiencies may not be there to rapidly and successfully deploy the process when it really counts. Thus, incident responders should use every opportunity to practice the *peacetime-to-wartime shift* and be comfortable enough that the use of the framework is not as chaotic as the incident itself.

If you always use IMS, regardless of how minor an issue may first appear, the framework and the Incident Commander are in place and ready to escalate if necessary.

Span of Control

As humans, we all have limits around how much information we can process at any given moment or how much attention we can pay to competing conversations or tasks, especially under stress. In peacetime, multitasking is commonplace. In wartime, incident responders should be mindful of not getting overwhelmed with too much data, too many simultaneous conversations, or too many tasks to complete in a compressed time frame. It is critical to recognize your limits and the limits of others, and not stretch to the point of breaking, especially when managing people under stress during an incident.

Span of control is the maximum number of people that one person can manage. Typically, that number is 5–7 people. Keeping an acceptable span of control ensures *unity of command*, or clear lines of reporting authority. When 30 people join an incident conference call bridge, with or without a defined leader, the conversation can quickly degrade, become unproductive, and lose focus, which wastes time that can never be recovered.

In simple terms, span of control is a management tactic for the Incident Commander. It's used when there is a need to organize many incident responders in a way that maintains control of the tasks being assigned and the discussions that must take place. It's breaking down a large set of tasks into smaller, more manageable activities and delegating the work in a way that allows the work to be tracked and managed efficiently.

This is not to say that the recommended span of control of 5–7 direct reports must never be violated. Remember that incidents are dynamic and can change, often quite rapidly and dramatically, but don't get caught with too large a span of control.

Let's review the concept of span of control in action with this example, using the CAN report format:

Conditions

- System performance has slowed after a recent software change in a critical application
- The cause is unknown

Actions

- Level 1 help desk has determined the problem is beyond their scope and escalated to the IRT

Needs

- IRT to investigate

Note

Again, in low-impact issues, it may be as basic as an Incident Commander leading a small group of only two or three incident responders, as seen in Figure 4-1. In this illustration, the organizational chart represents a small group of first responders (SMEs) to arrive on an incident conference call bridge: one DBA, one network engineer, a SAN/Storage engineer, and the Incident Commander.

As with any incident, the Incident Commander role is initially filled by the first qualified IC on the bridge. However, keep in mind that the function of Command may be transferred at any time to anyone for any reason as long as that person is qualified to fill the role of Incident Commander.

Even for this simple seeming incident response (low-severity, noncomplex), the position of Incident Commander should be established. Again, looking toward the fire service as a guide, you could hear something like this radio transmission on a regular basis, even on what might be considered a routine incident: "Engine 2 on scene of a two-vehicle traffic accident. Looks like all parties are out of the vehicles. Engine 2 establishing Oak Street Command." There are certainly variations on the words used, but the point is that even though this incident seems like a small green-yellow box issue, the fire service does it that way because it is *the way,* and when that same fire engine pulls up on a large incident, the process of establishing command is familiar and automatic.

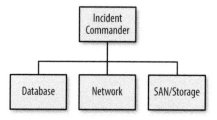

Figure 4-1. Simple command structure for a low-severity issues

You'll also notice in Figure 4-1 that the boxes aren't identified by the name of the person filling the position, rather only the job functions are named: IC, Database, Network, and SAN/Storage. Going back to the example just given about the fire service, the company officer (leader of the team) on Engine 2 didn't say, "Frank, Pete, Bill, and Kathy are on scene." They were identified by their function, which in this case it is a team function called Engine 2. As another example, the big ladder trucks you see at a fire represent a specific function, just as the hazardous materials response unit is a function, and so is a technical rescue team. To that point, the process of establishing command and directing resources by job function (SMEs) instead of by name of person allows for the organizational chart to grow quickly and clearly, even if the person filling the function changes for some reason. The function is the constant. The specific person who fills it may vary day to day, and even during an incident.

If more than one DBA is needed in the example shown in Figure 4-1, a database group can be created and the Incident Commander will only need to communicate with the leader of the database function (Database Group Leader, or DGL) without keeping track of the multiple individuals assigned to it. If your organization is small and everyone knows each other, this may seem ridiculous, but when the SME pool is large or spread around the globe, it's much clearer to keep track of your SMEs by function rather than name.

To continue with the example shown in Figure 4-1, assume that after a few minutes of discussion, three more DBAs from another time zone join the incident conference call bridge. The Incident Commander acknowledges the new incident responders that joined the bridge and the ensuing conversation might sound like this:

SME: "Hi this is Allen from database."

SME: "Kelly just joined as well."

Incident Commander: "Hi, Allen. This is Ben. I'm the Incident Commander and we are working a SEV 1. Thanks for joining. I also heard Kelly joined."

SME Kelly: "Yes, I'm a DBA in Sydney, Australia. I'm here with James as well."

Incident Commander: "Copy that, sorry to wake you at this hour, but we need your help. I'm in the middle of a conversation with the SAN/Storage engineer and will give you a CAN report shortly. Stand by for now."

SME: "Copy that. Stand by."

SME Kelly with James: "Okay."

In this quick exchange, the Incident Commander has laid out the rules of engagement for the SMEs to join the bridge, then must decide the timing of giving updates and/or engaging the SMEs. If an important conversation is in progress and a new person joins, the Incident Commander may wait to acknowledge the SME in favor of not breaking the flow of the conversation. There are no set rules on this. It is up to the Incident Commander how to manage the flow of incident responders arriving on the incident conference call bridge.

Additionally, some IRTs use a status page or some other way to electronically capture events and make the information available to all incident responders. This is an efficient way to provide status updates and up-to-the-minute information about the incident response. Absent that, however, the Incident Commander can provide CAN reports at regular intervals to keep everyone informed.

Let's fast forward and assume that our example of an incident response scenario is quickly increasing in severity and the number of incident responders has grown to nine. To prevent chaos on the bridge, the Incident Commander would need to maintain span of control. Let's assume that the incident is identified as a database issue and there is robust conversation occurring between the DBAs. Since there are now five DBAs on the call, and depending on what is being discussed on the bridge, it might make sense for the Incident Commander to:

1. Create a database group.

2. Assign one of the DBAs to the role of the Database Group Leader (DGL).

3. Direct them to set up another incident conference bridge and move their conversations to that bridge.

4. Ask that only the DGL report back to the Incident Commander and/or answer for the group.

The DGL may or may not be a peacetime database manager or even the most experienced DBA. In fact, it's totally the Incident Commander's choice (with DBA input and what's right for the situation), but the DBAs need to support their DGL.

The newly appointed DGL should take the following actions:

1. Move the database group from the main incident conference call bridge to a database-group bridge.

2. Lead the discussions on the database-group bridge.

3. Assign tasks to DBAs in the database group and facilitate discussions.

4. Report back to the Incident Commander on the main incident conference call bridge.

Figure 4-2 illustrates the organizational chart representing the newly formed database group. You can see that the Incident Commander is mindful of span of control by grouping the DBAs together.

Note

The Incident Commander can be creative with the command structure, but the idea is to delegate or chunk off the tasks in a way that keeps the number of people reporting to any other person within the 5–7 span of control range.

It's appropriate for the DGL to inform the Incident Commander of the results of the database group work and or recommendations/actions. In that discussion, the Incident Commander should direct questions to the DGL. Importantly, the DGL is the only person who speaks for the database group. If the database group is disbanded after the tasks are completed, everyone from the database group, including the DGL, are available for another set of tasks.

This is a simple illustration of the point, but with the modular nature of IMS, an Incident Commander can build out a structure to streamline and monitor/control the response more effectively. By grouping resources, appointing group leaders (GL), and assigning tasks by function, communication is direct and easier to follow. If another group of experts were needed, the Incident Commander could create another group with another name, appoint a leader, outline tasks with a timeline, and expect a report from the GL on the incident conference call bridge.

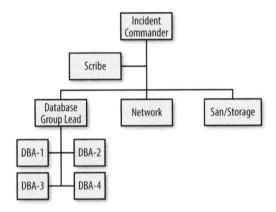

Figure 4-2. The incident organizational chart for an expanded incident

Additionally, you see the position of *scribe* (SitStat) is added to the organizational chart. It's also called SitStat because it's the function that keeps the situational status at all times during the incident. A scribe (whether it is a person performing the task or perhaps automated in some way) is useful to assist the Incident Commander with documenting: the incident responders; incident timeline; assignments made by function with time deadlines; and actions taken. Not all organizations have the luxury of a large IRT or a large pool of SMEs, so this position may not be realistic for your IRT. If not, scribing should still be done, but it gets done by the Incident Commander. You may be documenting the response electronically, which is certainly useful, but keep in mind that the scribe position is a great way for junior members of the IRT to gain experience and observe a more senior member handling an incident response. Additionally, scribing may be viewed as a mundane task, when in reality it is quite important in terms of keeping an accurate timeline of the incident and becomes the basis for an After Action Review (AAR).

Note

The scribe (SitStat) position is shown here as a function to be filled and doesn't count against the span of control for the Incident Commander. It is a supportive role and not active in problem-solving effort.

Figure 4-3 represents a possible way the example in Figure 4-2 might escalate with even more incident responders, still maintaining a proper span of control.

At this point, it's useful to define the term escalate. In IT, *to escalate* has two separate, but interrelated meanings: 1) to take an issue to a higher-ranking manager for a decision; 2) in the event a person identified as a primary on-call resource does not respond within a time frame, call the secondary or tertiary resource. Here's a typical dialogue for the first definition: "This is a network decision I don't have the authority to make, so I'm going to escalate to my network manager to make the call." Here's a typical dialogue for the second definition: "The primary network on-call was paged 15 minutes ago and hasn't joined the incident conference call bridge, so I'm going to escalate to the secondary on-call so we can get someone from network onto the bridge."

In the fire service, *to escalate* has a very different definition: to request *more* or *different* resources as conditions change on an incident. Here's a typical fire service dialogue from the Incident Commander: "Fire has spread to the second floor, dispatch a second alarm and two more ambulances."

We recommend using the fire service definition of *escalate* in IT. As we described earlier, MTTA is the only part of the incident response that the IRT can truly control. In the second definition of *escalate* in IT, a primary on-call incident responder is not responding, which is hindering the IRT from moving forward to resolve the incident, and wasting valuable time. As we discussed earlier, if an incident responder is available, they are in a position of operational readiness, will join an incident conference call bridge with a sense of urgency, and arrive able to complete assignments from the Incident Commander.

We had a client ask us "How does the fire department deal with a fire engine that is dispatched to a scene but doesn't show up?" We were flabbergasted by the question, because that situation never happens in the fire department! To be sure, fire engines get flat tires or break down and can't respond, but if they are available for incident response, they are in a position of operational readiness, will respond with a sense of urgency, and will arrive able to complete assignments from the Incident Commander. The nonresponsive primary on-call issue should be discussed with their manager off the incident conference call bridge to prevent this from occurring again.

Back to our example: The incident expanded quickly and the Incident Commander chose to increase the SEV level and call for the different resources, "I'm escalating this to a SEV 1. Let's get the Disaster Recovery Team (DR) team activated."

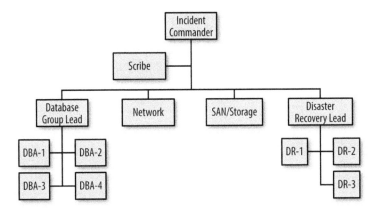

Figure 4-3. The incident organizational chart showing a greater expansion in the incident

When the DR team arrives on the bridge, the organizational chart would change accordingly. Again, more incident responders joined, but the span of control of the Incident Commander remained within an acceptable range. Figure 4-4 represents a further expansion of the IMS framework. Don't worry about understanding the job functions in terms of their specific duties for this scenario. Rather, focus on the organizational chart and how an expanding incident can accommodate a large number of incident responders by assigning groups. Functions like plans, liaison officer, and scribe are called *command staff functions* (assigned to assist the Incident Commander directly) and are not counted against the span of control. Again, the Incident Commander can configure the organizational chart to keep control over the resource pool and maintain an effective span of control.

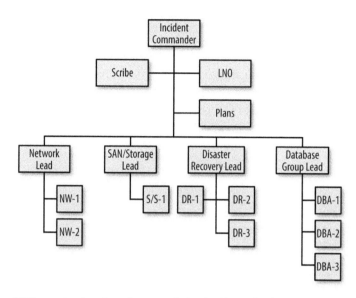

Figure 4-4. IMS organization chart for an escalating incident. This level of response may be indicated for red-box incidents.

Transfer of Command

If incidents go on for an extended period of time, command (as well as any of the other functions) can be transferred to another qualified member of the IRT. The transfer should be an orderly process and announced on the incident conference bridge. So, when is this done? Transferring command or any other job function can happen anytime during an incident response, but it most commonly occurs when:

- There is a natural break in a work period, such as shift changes or global handoffs between teams.

- An Incident Commander is fatigued and it's in the best interest of the incident to get a well-rested person into the position.

- An Incident Commander may be struggling and a more qualified person is available.

- For business reasons, a more senior or higher-ranking peacetime person should be leading the incident response.

As mentioned, the off-going Incident Commander should announce to the group that command is being transferred and introduce the new oncoming Incident Commander to the group. Prior to that, the off-going Incident Commander should provide a CAN report to the on-coming Incident Commander off the incident conference call bridge in order to bring that person up to speed on the current conditions and activities on the bridge. The reason this is done off the incident conference call bridge is so that the two Incident Commanders can have a candid conversation about the incident response efforts. If there is a problem SME that the off-going Incident Commander was not able to handle, they can discuss a strategy to deal with this situation. The off-going Incident Commander may have wanted to go another direction but the team was resistive. The new Incident Commander can come in and present the new plan and move it forward. When a new direction is needed, a change in Incident Commanders can facilitate this redirection.

Summary

In the world of public safety, some incidents are big and complex and require a lot of people to be coordinated and managed—like the World Trade Center incident on 9/11. Some incidents are relatively small and can be handled in most cases by a small team of incident responders—like a small house fire. A routine medical call requires a smaller incident response and would typically be handled by a smaller team of medical and fire personnel.

In IT, the IRT may be called upon to solve and recover from large, complex incidents, such as a widespread, persistent DDoS attack. High SEV incidents might require the collective problem-solving skills of network engineers, DBAs, key peacetime executives, outside vendors, and perhaps even a disaster recovery team, which may result in dozens of people cycling on and off an incident conference call bridge. Conversely, a handful of engineers may be working a problem with a single customer having an issue with an application.

- The best way to build skill and proficiency in incident management is to regularly use IMS for green and yellow box issues, not just on large, complex red- and black-box incidents.

- Each Incident Commander should strive to find the right mixture of command, framework, and problem-solving effort to create the most effective incident resolution environment, matched to the size and scope of the incident.

- *Span of control* is the maximum number of people that one person can manage. Typically, that number is 5–7 people.

- The *function of Command* (or any other job function on a response) may be transferred at any time to anyone for any reason as long as that person is qualified to fill the role.

- Job *functions* during an incident response are constant. The *people* who fill the function may vary.

5

Unified Command (UC)

Complex, high-severity incidents that create serious impact across multiple business units geographic territories or functional areas require an expanded version of IMS. These incidents generally need high-level business or policy decisions that will impact the entire business and are beyond the scope of an IC implementing IMS to resolve a technology incident. Unified Command is a group of senior business and technology leaders who establish a common set of objectives and strategies and a single incident action plan, which is implemented by the Incident Commander and IRT.

Larger companies, especially enterprise companies, may find challenges in communications and span of control when an incident involves multiple business units, functional areas, environments, or teams with unique—sometimes conflicting—goals (for example, operations and security) or any other kingdoms that exist within the organization.

The word *kingdom* in this context describes a business unit or other entity within a company. To that end, *Unified Command* (UC) is most effective when an incident requires engagement and communication among multiple kingdoms across the company.

Note
IMS is used to manage individuals and teams within a kingdom. UC is used to manage across kingdoms within an organization.

Not all companies will need to implement UC if incidents typically only involve a small number of incident responders, do not cut across kingdoms, or do not result in serious business impact. As you have seen previously, IMS is a flexible management framework that can be set up to fit any situation. UC is a meta framework used when the incident scales, requiring the responders to scale accordingly. The size, scope, and nature of the incident dictates how the management framework is used—not the other way around. As the name implies, UC provides a framework to make joint decisions during the incident when there are multiple competing interests. UC has the following characteristics:

- It's an advanced form of IMS.

- It's used in complex or large-scale incidents.

- It's valuable when multiple business units or functional entities must work together.

- It's typically activated for incidents requiring executive-level business or policy decisions.

- It consolidates information to establish a common set of objectives and strategies.

- When UC is activated, it is at the top of the IMS hierarchy. SMEs work for the Incident Commander, who works for the UC.

- Ultimately, UC is a tool to streamline inter-kingdom communications and incident resolution efforts under a single Incident Action Plan (IAP).

UC at its very core is about cooperation at the command level. It's an effective way to communicate on top of an incident response framework. Again, it may sound complicated at this point, but we will offer some advice and guidance on how to implement it in your organization.

Here are a couple of broad examples that may require UC activation:

- Situations where there are two or more technology options for incident resolution, but each has different business impact. The IRT can execute either plan, but executive engagement is required to make the best decision for the business. Those decisions must be communicated and/or carried out by one or more kingdoms. However, the executives should remain focused on their role as business/policy leaders and leave the Incident Commander and incident responders to do their jobs.

- Incidents where rapid communication and decision-making are required vertically or horizontally across the company and/or outside organizations (customers, regulators, etc.).

These are general examples, and there are so many things that may be unique to your company that it's best for us to focus on the UC framework and leave the specific triggers for activating UC to you. The activation of the UC model is determined by the organizational need and the Incident Commander handling the current problem. UC may be infrequently used, but when it's needed, it's a great tool for scaling a response to fit the needs of a complex problem.

The role of UC is to:

- Provide high-level coordination between entities and serve as a single point of contact for all business units involved in the response.
- Support and allocate resources to the Incident Commander.
- Communicate with senior executive levels and laterally to other business units as needed.
- Communicate down to the tactical level of the Incident Commander.
- *Above all,* do whatever needs to be done, such as using executive relationships to get more or different resources from either inside or outside of the company to help the Incident Commander run the incident and fix the issue.

UC in Action

During the early stages of an incident, Incident Commanders and the IRT must develop an initial Incident Action Plan (IAP). Frequently, this action plan must be developed very quickly based on incident size-up and initially may not be a complete plan to resolve the incident. It's common for an IAP to be a template for formulating the solution or a roadmap for information gathering. In some cases, the IAP starts out as a plan to make a plan for resolution.

Based on a good size up, the response effort may go down one of two paths. The first path is a typical response whereby standard IMS practices are employed. A common example is: a SEV 1 of short duration with customer impact; the business is not in a critically compromised state; the Incident Response Team is making progress; there is a high degree of confidence in resolving the problem; the SMEs are engaged and working for the Incident Commander until the incident is resolved. In short, it's a nasty incident but doesn't pose a large risk to the company's reputation, compromise the trust of its customers (internal or external) or investors, or appear to pose a serious financial threat of lost revenue or high cost of downtime.

The second path will build on the first path if the problem escalates to the point where other kingdoms within a company are involved or if the impact is such that there is a serious threat to the company, as defined by the company itself. If this is the case, the Incident Commander can activate UC, which will then be available to make high-level decisions for the business and to reach across kingdoms for resources/involvement/direction to support the Incident Commander. Beyond the technology problem, UC is about the business impact to the company that transcends solving the technology problem. Hence the word "Unified" in Unified Command.

It's possible that the UC Group, lead by a Unified Command Leader (UCL), may decide that an even higher level of executive support/involvement is required and elect to make a *Tier 1 notification*. This is another layer of support for the Incident Commander (and UC for that matter) and the rest of the incident resolvers. Again, UC and/or the Tier 1 On-Call Executive (OCE) groups are typically activated when a technology problem creates serious business impact. As an example, the incident resolvers may have two plans for resolution of a technology issue, each of them with unique consequences and impact on the business and may seek executive-level support in order to get direction regarding the best course of action *for the business*. The technology solution(s) may, in some cases, be straightforward, but the impact may be better understood by high-level peacetime executives who have a broader view of the business landscape than the Incident Commander and corps of SMEs.

In plain terms, an Incident Commander may present a situation to UC, in effect saying, "I have two solutions and I can pull this lever or that one with equal ease. Here are the pros and cons of each solution. Which one would you like me to implement?" This is a gigantic oversimplification but it should underscore the point. Incident responders respond and resolve. UC supports the Incident Commander. Executives provide high-level business and policy direction.

Again, the Tier 1 group is comprised of the highest-level executives in the company. The role of a Tier 1 group is to:

- Gather information relating to the incident from UC.

- Analyze and disseminate high-level relevant information inside and outside the company.

- Establish policy and priorities for the incident resolution effort.

- Interface with customers and outside vendors as deemed necessary.

- Support the incident resolution effort.

Upon recognition of a high-severity incident that may benefit from UC, the Incident Commander initiates the activation sequence for UC, as determined by the company. The triggers for that will vary widely, so it is up to you to identify under what circumstances UC makes sense.

It is up to the members of UC to initiate the upstream notifications to the Tier 1 group. Figure 5-1 depicts the hierarchical relationship between the SMEs, Incident Commander, UC, and Tier 1 group.

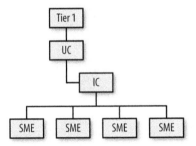

Figure 5-1. The hierarchical relationship between the SMEs, Incident Commander, UC, and Tier 1 group

The Unified Command management structure will allow teams to focus on their distinct roles and responsibilities to manage their own piece of the response while executing a common IAP with resource coordination, information-sharing, and decision-making. The structure can expand or contract to meet the specific needs of a situation. Figure 5-2 offers a logic path for activating the UC Group and/or Tier 1 and provides a quick reference for examples of activation triggers and job functions.

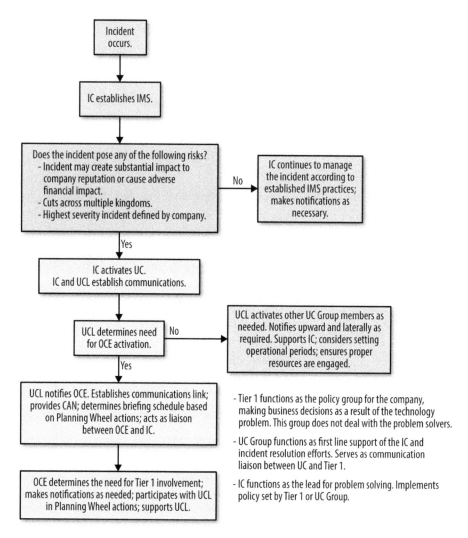

Figure 5-2. A logic path for activating the UC Group and/or Tier 1, and quick reference for examples of activation triggers and job functions

The UC Planning Wheel

When UC and/or Tier 1 is activated, the process of plan development, notifications, and briefings, as outlined in Figure 5-3, begins. These initial notification/mobilization/briefing actions form the supporting base of the *UC Planning Wheel*. The UC Planning Wheel is a depiction of the series of notifications, briefings, and interactions that occur between the Incident Commander, UC, and the Tier 1 group. Remember, not all UC activations require the involvement of Tier 1, but we chose to add them into the illustration to show you a fully built out incident process. Like everything else in IMS, the rules are flexible, and should be adapted to the situation. UC is commonly activated in the fire service for larger incidents or when multiple agencies (law enforcement, fire department, and emergency medical services, etc.) work together on the same incident.

In the fire service, just like in IT, as the severity and impact of an incident grows, so does the support and involvement of higher and higher levels of leadership within the organization. The higher levels of leadership are not there to resolve the issue, but to provide guidance and support to the Incident Commander and other resolvers. A good analogy can also be found in professional sports. When the game is on the line, the owner of the team does not come down onto the field, put on a jersey, and start playing. The owner works with the coach (Incident Commander) and players (SMEs) to figure out a game plan to win.

Once the UC Group enters the Planning Wheel (indicated by the arrow), a series of informational exchanges and briefings occur. These interactions are intended to help clarify and direct operational priorities and actions to be carried out by the Incident Commander and/or other incident responders tasked with solving the problem.

It's been said many times but cannot be over emphasized: the Tier 1 group and UC aren't charged with solving the problem—that's the job of the Incident Commander and SMEs. Additionally, the Planning Wheel depicts the points where informational exchanges or briefings can occur during an operational period. *Operational periods* are set jointly by the Incident Commander, UC, and Tier 1 (if activated), depending on the severity and needs of the incident.

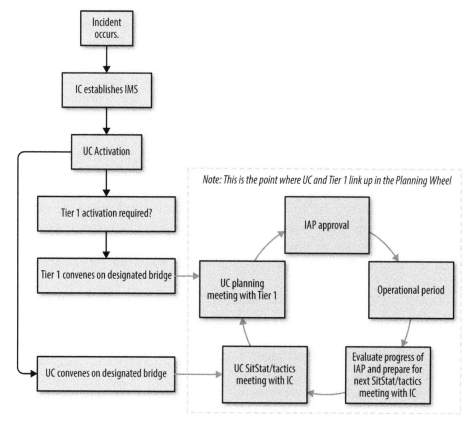

Figure 5-3. UC Planning Wheel

Note

Operational periods are time periods established by the Incident Commander and the IAP and establish blocks of time for meeting the established objectives defined in the IAP. As an example, if a rolling restart is the determined course of action, the Incident Commander would determine how long this operation will take to complete. During the CAN report, the Incident Commander can announce: "We are doing a rolling restart which will take an hour, so we will have another operational brief when that is completed." That period of time is known as the operational period. Another option is that the Incident Commander can set a two-hour operational period and at the end of that period, if the incident is not resolved, it would trigger additional resources to be dispatched or executives to be notified.

The UC Group can cycle through the Planning Wheel quickly or slowly, depending on incident needs. There are no hard-and-fast rules for the cadence of briefings and information exchange. The key point is to set up the communications protocol so that the incident resolvers have quick access to guidance and direction from UC and/or Tier 1 (if activated). Conversely, the Incident Commander should keep UC and Tier 1 well informed on a timely basis.

Warning

The UC and the Tier 1 group should not implement problem-solving actions without including the Incident Commander and/or other groups actively engaged in problem-solving. No group in the system should be out of the loop or take independent action from the consolidated Incident Action Plan.

PLANNING WHEEL IN ACTION

As depicted in Figure 5-3, the starting point for planning and communications on the Planning Wheel is the initial Situation Status (SitStat) briefing between the Incident Commander and UCL; when several persons are convened in UC, a single person from that UC Group is identified as *Unified Command Lead* (UCL). There is more explanation on the members of UC later. It is "Unified," so there must be more than one person to unify with!

The UCL is the function that keeps the UC Group on task and moving forward, much like an Incident Commander or functional group leader does. The interaction between the UCL and Incident Commander is where both entities quickly get the lay of the land and a general sense of the problem. There may be no specific action plan identified at this point, and perhaps not all responders are engaged, but an initial problem statement is formed to the degree that UC can get an idea of the scope and severity of the problem and/or whether the Tier 1 group should be activated.

From there, if Tier 1 is convened, the UCL notifies them and provides a CAN report to the Tier 1 on-call executive (OCE). If UC is something you think works for your company, we strongly suggest you have 24×7×365 access to the functions of UCL and OCE. This will speed up the MTTA for UC and get the right people together much more quickly. Again, this initial interaction may be more of a cursory report or notification based on a rapid size-up of the situation, or perhaps there is a clear understanding of the problem and potential solution sets. In any case, the OCE then determines the need for further notifications at the executive level. It may be that the OCE remains the sole point of contact for UC. In any case, the early involvement of Tier 1 via the OCE is key if UC believes there will be a need for high-level executive engagement.

The next step, if and when enough information is known, is to approve, recommend, or provide direction back through the UCL to the Incident Commander on any business-level decisions made and other policy-level directions for the Incident Commander and SMEs. The UC should also disseminate appropriate information to peers across the kingdoms and ensure that the Incident Commander is clear on the desires of the Tier 1 group. That information is acted upon during an operational period (which could last anywhere from minutes, to hours, to days or weeks) and then reevaluated by the Incident Commander and the IRT, who then feed back into the Planning Wheel with a SitStat report back to the UCL.

All along the Planning Wheel, there may be assignments or information given and received to other business units or individuals that report back to the Incident Commander, UCL, or OCE as appropriate. The wheel spins as fast as it needs to keep up with the needs of the incident. The UCL becomes a pivotal person in the process, interfacing with the Incident Commander and the OCE and/or representatives from Tier 1. The UCL function should be filled by a person with enough power and rank in the organization to "make things happen" for the IC.

As with other elements of IMS, the members of UC and Tier 1 can change from incident to incident, but the identified functional roles remain the same, as does the workflow and communications channel. This makes the process repeatable (the "R" in PROCESS from Chapter 1) because the functions are clearly identified, no matter who is participating.

UC Org Chart

Figures Figure 5-4 and Figure 5-5 provide an overview of the relationship between the Incident Commander, Unified Command, and the Tier 1 group.

Figure 5-4 is a simple representation of UC as it relates to the Incident Commander. Typically, a single Incident Commander takes command of the incident, even when it may involve different business units. The group leaders (GL)—in this case, from Site Reliability, Application 1, Application 2, and a DEV team—coordinate the actions of their group and pass information and needs to the Incident Commander using CAN reports. In turn, the Incident Commander coordinates and creates a line of communication and briefing schedule with UC, more specifically with the UCL. The SMEs carry out tasks assigned by the Incident Commanders and work directly with their group leaders.

The important point to recognize is that in basic IMS, the Incident Commander is managing single resources (SMEs) in the incident reponse organization chart. When UC is activated, the Incident Commander will still be in charge of the incident response effort, but each particular business unit becomes responsible for their group, which then reports up to the Incident Commander and ultimately to UC.

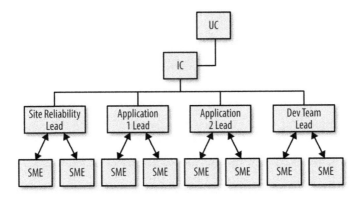

Figure 5-4. UC as it relates to the Incident Commander

When the SEV of the incident requires the involvement of Tier 1, the UCL contacts the OCE and makes the notification. The UCL should pass along as much information as is known at the time and establish a briefing schedule for CAN reports. This link between UC and Tier 1 is vital to ensure that information, by whatever medium is chosen, can be passed along as quickly as possible. If an Incident Commander is considering a course of action, or several courses of action, that may have reputational or business impacts beyond his or her authority, it is crucial to get the input/approval up to UC and to Tier 1 and back down again as soon as possible. Secondarily, the UC Group may need to make lateral notifications or solicit assistance for the Incident Commander through another business unit on behalf of the Incident Commander. Figure 5-5 illustrates the incident organizational framework for Tier 1 when it is activated.

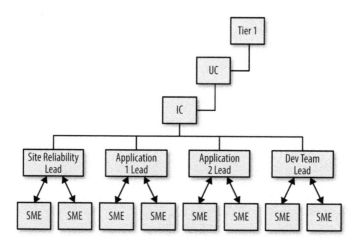

Figure 5-5. The incident organizational framework for Tier 1 when activated

Keep in mind that these examples are used to illustrate the concept of UC, not to specify how it is to be used in your company during an incident. IMS is a flexible management framework and should be implemented in such a way that it is matched to the requirements of the incident.

UC Case Study

In previous chapters, we discussed the need for pre-planning of planned events. Developing an IAP for new code releases is important because it establishes, in advance of the release's implementation, who will be in charge if the release goes sideways and turns into an incident.

In the following case study, the company did not pre-plan, so the response was delayed until an incident was declared and the incident response started. The company was pushing a new code release. The release team followed standard change-management procedures, and checked with the operations team prior to launching the release. The operations team approved the launch, and the release team launched the code.

The release went well at first, but then servers started crashing. A number of alerts popped up in the operations team's monitoring tools, so they declared an incident and opened an incident conference call bridge. The monitoring tools did not indicate that the release went sideways, only that servers were crashing. The operations team was not sure at this point of the actual cause. The release team was actively trying to figure out what went wrong. The two teams were not communicating, which hampered the incident resolution efforts.

Finally, the operations team checked the logs, determined that the release was the likely suspect, and brought the release team into their response. After some initial wrangling, the operations team assumed the Incident Commander role and started making assignments and working on a plan to restore service. The incident response was getting organized, with the various roles filled out. The IRT had an Incident Commander, a scribe, an liaison officer (LNO; see sidebar), and SMEs (DBA GL, network, storage, app engineers, and the release GL). Figure 5-6 provides an overview of the initial structure.

The Role of the LNO

The *LNO* acts as an aide to the Incident Commander for communications between the various groups and/or bridges and other communications channels. The LNO stays connected and fully up to speed with the Incident Commander, understanding the incident in the same way as the Incident Commander and able to deliver a CAN report on a moment's notice.

The function of the LNO is to move (liaison) between communications channels, providing updates and briefings on behalf of the Incident Commander and gathering information from those channels to bring back to the Incident Commander. The LNO is the mobile eyes and ears of the Incident Commander, which allows for the Incident Commander to stay focused and connected to the problem-solving effort and main communications channel (oftentimes a conference call bridge). The Incident Commander may set a briefing schedule for the LNO to make the rounds to those outside the main problem-solving effort. Any group of responders may assign the LNO position for the purpose of intergroup communications.

Think of the LNO as a deputy Incident Commander. The LNO speaks on behalf of the Incident Commander, but doesn't make decisions for the Incident Commander. Effective LNOs have a version of command presence. They will give and get briefings with the confidence that "there is no question I can't answer or get the answer to."

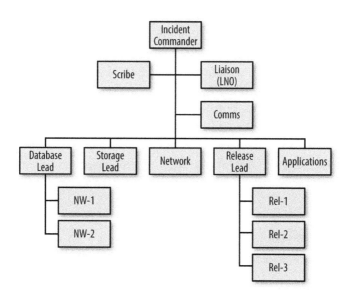

Figure 5-6. The organizational chart for the IRT

The Incident Commander was able to guide the discussion to several poten-tial paths forward, but some options had more risk than others. Very quickly, the SMEs were able to determine that one of the options to restore service may involve data loss, and they were not sure at that point whether or not any data had already been lost. The Incident Commander decided that any future deci-sions would most likely have substantial business impact and wanted to get some additional executive support. The path with the least amount of risk also had the least chance of success. The path that had the best chance of success carried a lot of risk and there was some potential for data loss. The Incident Commander reviewed the potential paths forward with the other SMEs and they all agreed the risky path was the best one.

The Incident Commander decided that since there was potential for adverse business impact—worse than what was currently being experienced—it was appropriate to activate Unified Command. The UCL joined the incident confer-ence call. Quickly, after receiving the initial CAN report from Incident Commander, the UCL decided to call for the vice president of infrastructure and representatives from legal, marketing, crisis communications, customer support, and security. UCL kept the span of control at 6. Each representative was an executive-level person. The group would form the initial UC Group as each busi-ness unit had an interest in the resolution effort. The UC would discuss and work through the business-impact decisions, while the incident conference bridge continued to work on problem-solving and determining the path-forward options. The UC Group not only discussed the potential paths forward but also customer notifications, including language for external postings and internal notifications. Each member of UC expressed their concerns with the proposed actions. The legal representative provided information on SLA or other potential contractual and legal concerns. The UCL was of the opinion that the OCE should be notified.

Meanwhile, the Incident Commander established the LNO role on the technical bridge and provided a briefing in a CAN report. The LNO dialed into the UC bridge (the bridges are separate so as to keep the technical bridge free of distractions). LNO relayed to the UCL that the Incident Commander would have a more defined resolution plan in 15 minutes and the LNO would then provide an update and some proposed paths forward. The LNO departed the UC bridge. Just after the LNO departed the UC bridge, the OCE joined the UC bridge and was briefed by the UCL. Afterwards, the OCE jumped off the UC bridge, made some notifications of his peer group of executives and returned to the UC bridge. Fifteen minutes later, the LNO returned to the UC bridge and presented to resolution options (this can be done by the Incident Commander as well, it just depends on the situation). The LNO presented the risks associated with the options, their chance of success, and the known length of time each would take. The UC Group asked a few questions and let the LNO know that the UC would discuss the options and get back to the LNO in 10 minutes. The LNO returned to the incident conference call bridge and gave the Incident Commander a CAN report on the interaction with UC.

The UCL then leads a discussion of the options with the UC Group and the OCE. The goal is to determine which option available to the Incident Commander presented the least amount of business impact, with the least amount of risk. The questions posed to the UC Group related to data loss and the potential to recover the data. The SMEs who could answer the questions of the UC Group were the database group, working under the Incident Commander. The LNO returned to the UC bridge at the appointed time. The UC Group asked the LNO to discuss their questions/concerns with the Database Group Leader (DGL) provide an answer back to them in 10 minutes. The LNO took that request back to the technical bridge. The DGL provided the answers to the Incident Commander and rest of the technical bridge, and the Incident Commander directed the LNO to provide this information to the UCL. Once the information was passed to the UC Group, they discussed and determined a course of action, clarified it with the LNO, and directed the LNO to also inform the Incident Commander that the group wanted an update when they had new information. The LNO returned to the technical bridge and provided another CAN report to the Incident Commander and the GLs. The SMEs took the action and for the most part, the action was successful. There was some functionality that did not fully restore and was still in a performance degradation state. The SMEs determined a workaround and established a timetable for full restoration. The LNO reported this information to the UCL.

Of course, this is a mythical scenario intended to illustrate the function of Unified Command, not represent the exact steps of solving a problem, so don't get too focused on anything other than the process. It may seem slow as you read through this, but in practice and with practice it is a very effective management tool.

The key takeaways are that each of the kingdoms within the UC were discussing items that were well above the concerns of the Incident Commander. The UC makes the big business-impact decisions and the Incident Commander directs the problem-solving efforts to carry out the directives of the UC. The Incident Commander would not have the bandwidth to handle both efforts, nor would the UCL have the ability to direct both the IRT and the UC Group. Once UC is activated, the UC handles strategic concerns and the Incident Commander handles tactical objectives.

Launching UC: The Programmatic Backend

So far, this chapter has looked at the nuts and bolts of UC. A few additional key points that largely exist in the background but are critical for the success of a UC activation include:

- In order to have a good MTTA for UC, you must identify all the key players that will make up the UC and how/when they are to be dispatched.

- Define trigger points for activation of UC and Tier 1.

- Identify methods of dispatch for UC and Tier 1 members.

- Predetermine UC and Tier 1 communication channels and/or protocols.

- Train all possible participants on their roles and responsibilities.

- Evaluate the performance of all UC activation participants after each response.

- Learn from each activation and constantly refine the response mechanism.

The success of UC, and IMS for that matter, are spelled out by the acronym PROCESS (see Chapter 1). IMS and UC are largely successful due to all the work that goes into setting up an incident response program prior to the actual incident response. When initial training matures into a bona fide incident response program and eventual culture change for the organization, it is easy to see that a healthy and well-organized response program is the key to successful incident response.

A poorly organized and insufficiently supported IRT will have trouble being successful with UC, much less being successful using IMS in general. This is because so much time is lost due to confusion between dispatch and notification, inefficient dispatch and notification processes, unclear roles and responsibilities, and too many communication channels that can't link together during an incident response. Look at any fire department that is considered a top-notch organization and you will find a robust organizational foundation in which there is clarity on who does what, when, and how. There is no ambiguity on what happens before the incident response. This sets up a strong take-off sequence for the transition from peacetime to wartime, which includes alerts identifying an incident, to the establishment of command, to the problem-solving effort.

There is an old adage in the fire service that goes like this: "As the first hoseline goes, so goes the fire." Translated, this means that if the first arriving fire unit sizes up the situation correctly and deploys the first tactical strike on the fire in an organized fashion (including establishing command), the probability of success for all subsequent actions increases. We know this isn't a universal constant, but after decades of experience fighting fires, we can tell you it is more true than not!

We frequently hear that teams use an incident conference call bridge for main communications, but that side conversations are happening via text, phone call, and chat group, which never get linked back to the main bridge or main communication tool. We suggest that you spend considerable time outlining the rules of engagement for the team (during peacetime) down to a painful level of detail when it comes to the frontend of the Incident Lifecycle. You will be glad you did, and will recognize a tremendous time savings when the bullet points listed at the beginning of this section are fully fleshed out.

KEY UC POSITIONS AND CHECKLISTS

Three key leadership positions exist in UC, and we will offer some thoughts on the job description and function of each. You are welcome to modify any of this to meet your individual needs. Our goal is to provide a starting point to work from.

- Unified Command leader (UCL)

- On-call executive (OCE)

- Group leader (GL)

Unified Command leader (UCL)

The UCL is a position that is on-call 24x7 and serves as the leader of UC Group when UC is activated and staffed by more than one person. The UCL position can be rotated during the week to spread out the responsibility of 24x7 coverage and can be transferred to other UC members if appropriate. The UCL stays on duty in the UCL position until UC is deactivated or the position is transferred. The UCL has the following characteristics and responsibilities:

- UCL receives activation notice initiated by Incident Commander.

- Responds to designated communications channel and receives CAN report from Incident Commander.

- Determines if additional UC members are required.

- Establishes UC communications bridge (if needed).

- Determines the need for OCE notification:

  — If OCE is notified, UCL makes contact as soon as possible to provide CAN report (see Figure 5-3).

  — If OCE is not notified, UC Group serves as the overhead management team for the Incident Commander.

  — UCL provides direction to Incident Commander as needed and notifications to the OCE as required.

- Leads the UC Group.
- Maintains communications between Incident Commander and OCE.
- Sets briefing cadence (if needed).
- Communicates horizontally across business units, etc. as needed.

On-call executive (OCE)

The OCE is a position that is on-call 24x7 and serves as the executive-level liaison between the Tier 1 group and UC Group. The OCE has the following characteristics and responsibilities:

- Receives activation notice from UCL.
- Responds to designated communications channel and receives CAN report from UCL.
- Determines if additional Tier 1 members are required.
- Establishes Tier 1 bridge or other communication method including EOC activation.
- Participates in Planning Wheel activities as depicted in Figure 5-3.
- Maintains communications with UCL.
- Sets briefing cadence for executives and others (if needed).

Group leader (GL)

The GL is a position that is on-call 24x7. The GL serves as the incident response leader and coordinator of a business unit, application, or other corporate or functional team within the company. Group leaders organize SMEs, technical experts, or others within the group as requested or directed by the Incident Commander or UCL.

The Incident Commander and/or UCL assign the GL position(s). When IMS is established for an incident or UC is activated (see Figure 5-4). There may be more than one group working with the Incident Commander and/or UC during any incident. The GL has the following characteristics and responsibilities:

- Activated and assigned by Incident Commander or UC (or formed at the Tier 1 level).

- Reports to designated communications channel, announces arrival, and receives CAN report from Incident Commander or UCL.

- Participates in problem-solving effort as directed.

- GL and team remains engaged with the incident until released by Incident Commander or UCL.

Summary

Most large businesses have many different business units spread across different geographic regions of the world. IT is the way these disparate groups communicate, collaborate, and conduct business with each other and their customers. When an incident occurs in these environments, it can have wide-scale impacts to the overall business. Incidents present themselves as technology issues, but they are really business issues.

When more than one business entity or group (aka *stakeholder*) within a company has joint responsibility to resolve an incident and must coordinate the efforts of many different SMEs, executives, application owners, outward-facing customer service groups, etc., UC is the best framework. When unique kingdoms have a stake in the game, the different stakeholders must share the role of command while working together to solve the problem.

- Unified Command (UC) is most effective when an incident requires the involvement and communication between multiple kingdoms from across the company.

- UC is a way to share the role of determining the best business resolution to an incident when there are competing interests at stake.

- UC is established to assist the Incident Commander to reach across business units to resolve a situation that may require some level of executive support. If an incident becomes larger or more complex, the UC Group may decide that even higher-level executive support is required and elect to make a Tier 1 notification.

- The UC Planning Wheel is an effective tool for thinking through how the UC Group functions.

- The Tier 1 group is comprised of the highest-level Executives within the company.

- The Tier 1 group and UC aren't charged with solving the problem! Their respective roles provide support and direction when the technology problem presents high-impact business consequences.

6

After Action Review (AAR)

Simply put, after the incident is resolved, there are two key areas to evaluate: 1) what broke? and 2) how did the people respond to what broke? To that end, instituting a comprehensive incident review process is a critical step in maximizing future uptime. Without doubt, identifying the cause(s) and or contributing factors of a technology failure are important, as the technology failure provides an opportunity to learn about the operating environment, make improvements, and fine-tune the IRT response mechanism to minimize future IT downtime. More importantly, establishing a positive culture around an honest and in-depth evaluation of the human part of the incident response is critical to improving how the people will engage and perform on future incidents.

Note

Don't let a good crisis go to waste! Learn from it to be better the next time. It's all about getting better—not finding blame.

The Name Is Important

There are some in the IT industry who refer to the incident review process as a *post mortem*. This term was associated with incident reviews because just as a post mortem searches for the cause of a person's death, the incident review searches for the cause of the technology's failure. In our opinion, post mortem is not the best term to use for evaluating an incident response or trying to determine the cause of an IT problem. For starters, when evaluating the performance of people, let's avoid using words typically associated with death! Post mortem certainly is retrospective, but it is also limited in scope. In fact, many people view post mortems as exercises in "searching for the guilty" and "standing in front of a firing squad," with organizations publicly shaming their employees for a technology failure.

Note

Establishing a positive, blameless culture of post-incident evaluation is based on an honest and in-depth evaluation of the incident response. It signals to the organization that technology failure is the perfect opportunity to learn about your operating environment and make improvements to minimize future IT downtime.

Along the same lines of a post mortem, many companies use *Root Cause Analysis* (RCA) as a term for investigating technology failure. In many cases, there may be more than one cause of the technology issue, so trying to identify one root cause is oversimplifying the analysis. As with post mortem, RCA is mainly focused on the technology failure ("the thing that broke"), which again does not lend itself to a wider view of evaluating other facets of the incident. In either case, the typical post mortem/RCA process has a hyper focus on the cause of the technology issue or contributing factors. What's commonly missing from an RCA or post mortem, however, is an evaluation of the people part of the incident response. For example, the way in which the IRT assembled or investigated the issue or solved the problem might have been inefficient for a number of reasons, causing the incident to last hours beyond what it should have. Perhaps there was a delay in the dispatch of the responders or arrival of SMEs, or the resolution effort wasn't effectively led by the Incident Commander. In any case, it's important to look at the contributing factors that may have prevented the incident responders from arriving at a quicker resolution. Think about this: if a certain IT problem took two hours to resolve, does it mean it was a two-hour problem because of the complexity of the problem or does it mean it took two hours to resolve because there was no process in place to manage and lead the human resources?

Again, any company that values IT uptime should continuously strive to reduce mean time to repair (MTTR). Of course, it's vital to have baseline statistics on incident response and MTTR in order to measure improvement. This is why having answers to the questions posed in Chapter 2 are so important.

Note

When done right, After Action Reviews protect the business. Evaluating past performance can help to prevent future incidents and improve the performance of the people.

This chapter will use the term *After Action Review* (AAR) as an alternative to post mortem. It's a more comprehensive (including technology *and* people) *review after* the *action* was taken. AAR casts a wide net across the entire incident, and it even has two A's in it—a good way to set the table for getting good grades!

According to John Allspaw, chief technology officer at Etsy, "The value of an AAR (or similar debriefing structure) is clear. In order to make them valuable (and not damaging) to future improvement (in terms of detection, response, prevention, etc.), explicitly declare and set the expectation that the debrief is about exploring multiple descriptions of the event. It's not about explanation—it's about description. Complex events require exploration with an open mind. As facilitators of debriefings, if we start questions with 'why,' we typically get an explanation from people involved with the event. We do not want explanations," he cautions, "we want descriptions. When we start questions with 'how' or 'what' or 'when,' then we get much more data during a debrief. There is never a 'One True Objective Account' of an event, only an amalgam of perspectives. Real learning comes from triangulating multiple perspectives, and that means that an AAR must set the conditions to collect and explore as many perspectives as it can, and avoid simplistic explanations, which can be tricky to avoid. So the forming of exploratory questions is really key to a successful AAR. Once we have these descriptions, then we have a good shot at turning that data into fruitful recommendations for the future."

Figure 6-1 depicts a typical Incident Lifecycle and how to think about integrating AAR and RCA into your thinking about incident response. You'll see that AAR links back to how the people responded and RCA feeds back into addressing the technology failure and how it might inform the company about reducing the same or similar problems in the future. For clarity, from here through the rest of the chapter, when we refer to AAR, we are also talking about the RCA part as well.

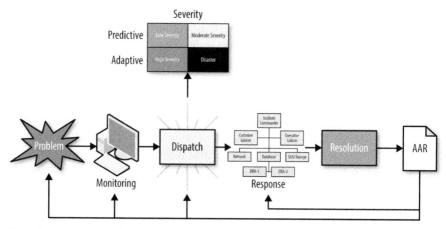

Figure 6-1. A typical Incident Lifecycle

AAR as an Integrated Effort

Whether it's a formal system based on IMS or ITIL/ITSM standards, DevOps, or a homegrown system, incident management will always involve human decision-makers, and people aren't perfect. Sometimes they make great decisions based on great information, and in some cases they follow gut instincts to good or not-so-good outcomes. Incident responders may catch or miss critical pieces of information during the Incident Lifecycle. In most cases, valuable lessons can be learned from each incident response—or at least they should be learned. In any event, an AAR can be viewed as a collection of lessons learned from each incident. Figure 6-2 shows where AARs fit into the relationship between the incident response and the evaluation of the response.

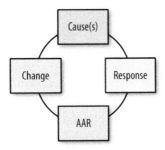

Figure 6-2. Perhaps the best way to describe where AARs fit in is to distill the relationship between the response and evaluation into its most basic parts: the cause of the technology failure, the people response to the incident, the AAR, and the process of change that is identified in the prior three parts

The change step in evaluating the incident response is where the feedback loops gets closed. Remember, incidents are resolved during wartime, but change occurs during peacetime. Honest evaluation allows incident responders and the company to learn from the incident and be better prepared for the next incident, and the one after that, and every one that happens in the future. Nothing reinforces a good lesson like feeling the thrill of getting it right—or the sting of getting it wrong, again.

The kinds of lessons learned from incidents are as varied as the incidents themselves:

- Maybe a certain incident helped the business see a blind spot in its architecture or service delivery.

- Perhaps some mistakes were made in detecting the problem and thus somebody learned a cool new trick with the monitoring or alerting tools.

- Perhaps a junior member of the IRT was covering the shift for a senior person, handled a tough event, and gained valuable experience and confidence as an Incident Commander.

- Perhaps a person or team chronically misses established incident response service level agreements (SLAs), thereby slowing the MTTA.

The list could go on and on, but one thing is for sure—the lessons are there. The real challenge most companies face is doing something productive with the answers.

It seems so simple. Why then do many companies find AARs to be such a challenge? Typically, it's about time and priority. For busy operations teams, they may be responding to the next incident and unavailable. Most operations teams work a shift schedule to provide incident response coverage, including weekends, while most SMEs work during normal business hours. Convening an AAR meeting that includes all incident responders on a specific incident can be challenging because of scheduling issues. Most companies don't have all the incident records (logs, recordings of communications, scribe information from the incident, etc.) in one spot, and assembling it may be challenging. Further, successful AARs require preparation, such as the compiling the incident timeline, roster of incident responders, organization of the responders, and discussion of possible resolutions. Many companies may not have resources to gather all that data for a comprehensive AAR.

On top of those challenges, teams within companies have competing interests: marketing and sales want new and improved things to sell, developers want to design new products, operations teams want stable environments, investors want growth, and executive management teams are charged with delivering results. Along with this, the operating environment is continually changing, from capacity planning of new elements in the stack to accommodate anticipated growth to refreshing old technology, all the while new code is being continuously released into production. Suffice to say, the people responsible for keeping the production environment running are crazy busy. Operations must keep all the balls in the air, all the time! Being in operations is like being a goalkeeper on a soccer team—they only remember the ones that get past you, not all the wonderful saves you made along the way.

Having said that, the focus of this chapter is about the wider view that is obtained through an AAR process, and why taking the time to do it is useful. But first, a word on why "playing the blame game" undermines an organization's ability to do an honest and genuine AAR.

Note

Instituting a process and, more importantly, establishing a culture of incident response and honestly evaluating all facets of an incident will cause you to look at risk differently. By examining all the potential causes of risk, you can determine where your risk lies: technology (hardware, software) processes, or your people responding to incidents. Many companies focus on the technology, but the incident response process or how people manage the incident may be where the biggest risk exists.

Let's just start by saying that playing the blame game is the primary deal killer in an AAR process. Sadly, it's easy to play and difficult to avoid, especially when you aren't the one in the hot seat. It's safe to say that most companies don't consciously start out looking to assign blame for a failure, but it seems easy for it to end up that way. It is not uncommon for an AAR (especially for a high-impact event) to end up as a witch hunt by looking for something or somebody upon which to pin the blame for the failure. Nobody likes to get criticized for making an honest mistake, and if the culture of the company is to make it uncomfortable for those responsible for failure, no matter how serious the problem, beware! It's only a matter of time before the harsh light of "You screwed up" is focused on you. We don't want to belabor this point, but a culture of fear or retribution of any kind is not productive and will ultimately stymie any effort to truly learn lessons from failures or mistakes.

There is, however, a big difference between a critique and being critical, and AARs shouldn't turn a blind eye to mistakes. It's more about the way they get pointed out and placed in context of the overall operations environment. So, an AAR is more of a critique rather than criticism, with the latter generally perceived as negative and oftentimes not accepted well by the receiver. When done well, a critique can provide excellent learning and growth opportunities while avoiding the blame game.

In order to set the table for true constructive feedback of incident responder performance, the culture of the company has to foster trust and respect among team members and allow mistakes to be made and learning to take place. Absent that, incident responders will likely choose only safe solutions to IT problems due to fear of being criticized if they're wrong. This stifles creativity, and part of being a good problem-solver is to see many different angles to a problem and deploy (sometimes) unconventional measures to correct them. Your operating environment is probably so complex that it would be next to impossible for any one person to know the entire technology stack in peacetime. Therefore, in wartime, the IRT must believe just that: they are not just a group—they are a team, assembled because they are good at what they do and there to support each other during the incident response.

AAR Documentation and Data Collection

If a culture of reviewing incidents, including evaluation of the incident response, doesn't exist in your organization, creating it can be challenging and very frustrating. However, the adoption and use of IMS will provide a standardized process and create a set of expectations that can assist with evaluating the human aspects of the incident response. Think of it this way—if you don't have a standardized way of responding to incidents, and, subsequently a method in place to evaluate the response and responders, how can you ever know if you are getting better?

When you document the various aspects of an AAR against a known set of criteria, it's easy to see where improvements can be made. Using standardized metrics creates a consistent process to manage incidents and measure responses. (Many of these metrics can be identified/developed by answering and collecting information on the type of questions posed in Chapter 2). If IMS was used in one incident but not another, comparing metrics will not be meaningful.

Here's a simple rule of thumb: the longer the time interval between the incident and the evaluation, the harder it is to convene an AAR and the less relevant the findings.

Ideally, the AAR is completed and the results finalized within a week of the event (and even that's too long!). This is a challenge for sure, but in order to link the incident to the performance to the corrective action (if there is any), the time from the event to the AAR results must be a short as possible.

To that end, an integrated AAR (AAR+RCA) starts by collecting five basic pieces of information to describe the incident.

1) A description of the problem (symptoms)	*What happened?*
2) A brief description of the cause of the incident	*What caused/contributed to the problem? This is somewhat subjective and may be quite complex based on your environment. The intent is to capture what caused a change from uptime to downtime.*
3) Who responded to solve it, and what are the time stamps for their dispatch and arrival on the incident? Were the initial responders the right ones for the incident or was it necessary to escalate to more or different SMEs?	*Were the right people assembled in the right spot to make the right decisions at the right time?*
4) What solution was implemented?	*Did the incident responders choose the right solution?*
5) What was the MTTA for the right team of responders and what was the MTTR?	*How long did it take to assemble and solve the problem?*

Once all the baseline documentation is compiled, a person or team (not necessarily part of the incident response) should create a timeline for the event. This includes the beginning and end time of the incident, request and arrival times of SMEs, when key decisions were made, and when the incident was declared under control or called all clear, etc. The following case study serves as an example timeline for an incident.

Documenting an Incident: A Case Study

What follows is a timeline from an After Action Review of an audio recording of the person-to-person actions during a fictional outage, that starts at 2 hours and 30 minutes into a software release. The company for our case study is a startup that is set up for email-based marketing campaigns on an Oracle-based system, with several data centers and a global workforce. They use an incident conference bridge as the main communication channel for incident response along with Slack for group chat.

The goal of this fictional review is to illustrate an approach to documentation during an incident. Capturing timestamps, a summary of key events, and the discussions that take place to support the decisions made during an incident provides valuable insight in to how the people responded. We find that most companies focus on technology failures and in many cases, fail to accurately document how the incident responders performed during an incident.

TIMELINE

Note that the time format is hours:minutes:seconds.

02:30:00 The software release team and the operations team discuss that the release is now impacting service and should become an incident. Nothing formal is decided and no Incident Commander is identified. The release manager (Pete) is still functioning as the lead on the bridge.

02:31:00 An SME is asking to check the analytics. An unidentified person states that there is a problem on Server 24, and that this may be an email problem. The person also says there is a need to call the email application team. "On second thought," he says, "someone should definitely call them." The SME reports they are not able to log in and check the dashboard. An unknown voice asks, "Is something else failing?" One of the other SMEs was able to log in.

02:33:45 Neal from customer support is reporting that the dashboard is looking good.

02:34:01 Pete reports that the dashboard is displaying time-delayed analytics. "Is it possible it hasn't been updated yet?" He asks Jan to check on it. Jan asks, "We are checking on the email issue—is that right?"

02:35:00 Pete asks Jan, "How do the analytics look?" Jan reports all good but Server 24. There is a lot of uncontrolled group discussion on database issues. The discussion centers on node 1 being shut down. There is also general discussion on which database team should be contacted.

02:40:47 One of the SMEs that earlier dropped from the call rejoins. Two SMEs from different database teams join and only provide their names, not their function/teams. Pete does not know them, and asks if they see any problems. They ask for the reason they were called, and want to know what is going on. There are several minutes of discussion on the situation. Pete is still the leader of the call but has not assumed the position of Incident Commander. The SMEs announce to the bridge that their analytics are showing some problems. They would like to move some partitions, and there is some discussion on this action. Other SMEs offer some other suggestions.

02:44:27 Customer Service is reporting more customer tickets, and they are starting to pile up. Pete asks for more specifics. Seems to be related to Server 24 and Server 28. One of the SMEs asks, "Which servers are the customers on?

Does anyone know?" This will have to be investigated, but Pete does not make this an assignment to a specific function or person.

02:46:23 There is a lot of background noise with one of the bridge participants. It sounds like someone is working from home and there are children's voices in the background. One of the Network SMEs finally addresses the noisy SME on the phone. "Whoever is working from home," he says, "put your phone on mute now please. We can hear your kids." The discussion is disjointed.

Lots of varied discussion off the bridge.

02:48:22 One of the SMEs offers that there should be a script revision, and Pete says someone should go in and change host names, but it is not directed at anyone. The possibility that the host names may not have been correct in the release is brought up. There are a lot of frustrated comments made about another failed software release.

02:53:00 A number of people have dropped from the bridge as the software release team wanted an offline discussion. No one announced this meeting, and the release team including Pete just disappeared from the bridge. Currently there are only two SMEs on the bridge, and they are feeling the bridge may have been lost, they are confused as to what is going on and what to do. They decide to continue their discussion on the host name issue and hope that the others will dial back in.

02:54:23 One SME comes back on the bridge and says that others will come back in a couple of minutes.

03:00:21 Customer Service reports that one of their big customers, Acme Chemical Sales, is reporting that multiple users are not able to log in and place orders. There is some discussion as to whether this is related to this incident or whether another bridge should be opened. It is determined to open a separate bridge.

03:03:26 Customer Service suggests to Pete that this is a big problem and that he should make the appropriate notifications for a P1 (Priority 1) incident, which requires executive and customer notifications at varied intervals. Pete ignores the discussion.

03:05:41 An unidentified SME asks, "Have we let the customers know we are resolving the issue?" Pete says it is not resolved and there are still problems. Customer Service says we have an incident and we need to send the proper notifications.

03:12:54 The customer notifications have still not gone out. There is some discussion about whether this a performance degradation or a service disruption, but the customers are reporting they can't log in. Pete determines that he will keep it a performance degradation.

03:14:54 An SME reports that the analytics do not look too bad. The only person that hears and comments on this is one of the database engineers.

03:19:02 An email SME joins and there is a discussion about email issues and one of the servers misbehaving. Pete is not sure what the problem is. Pete is looking for Bill, one of the email SMEs.

03:29:11 Bill rejoins and says, "There are some problems, and we need to get the senior executive on the call."

03:39:25 One of the SMEs suggests disabling incoming email. In the current state, the email is being lost. There is some discussion, then someone says, "Disable it, then we can discuss it." Another unidentified bridge participant observes that the problem is only for Server 24. Joe said he needs to check Server 28 to make sure there are no problems there.

04:09:14 Email test failed for Server 24 and analytics as well.

04:19:20 Pete reports that the executive has been contacted. Pete reports there are some issues in the Main Street Datacenter (MSDC), which started about 06:20. Pete reports there is another bridge opened by the network group and they are talking about the Server 28 issue. An SME wants to move to the other bridge to look at the database issues. There is confusion as to who is going to handle database issues between the SMEs.

04:21:43 The executive, Paul, joins and asks for an update. Pete says, "After the software release, there are a couple of customers that are not able to log in." Paul chimes in, "This may be a metadata issue." One of the SMEs confirms. Additional discussion occurs about the script. Paul asks, "How long are we going to investigate this issue?" The discussion continues, but no one answers the question. Paul asks the question a second and third time. One of the SMEs offers a very longwinded discussion on the investigation and, after several minutes, the SME answers that it will be about 30 minutes. Paul directs the group to "not do the investigation and to take quick action to restore service. This will cause a service disruption, but if successful would offer a quick solution." Many of the SMEs want to do more investigation for 30 more minutes.

04:29:22 Another executive joins, and someone provides an overview. One of the SMEs wants to rerun the script. Someone asks how long that might take. An unidentified person thinks it will take 30 minutes. The executive says if there was a problem with the script, it won't solve the problem. We need to confirm that the script was correct.

04:46:22 Discussion on the two approaches to take to resolve the issue.

04:58:41 Pete asks both executives if they want the group to focus on resolving the issue or continue investigating. No answer from either one.

05:08:05 An SME says, "It appears that the script did not run correctly and that we should run it again." Some discussion on whether there is any harm in running the script again other than time. Discussion on the process to run the script.

05:15:52 Customer Service says there are seven cases now and that the customers are unable to log in.

05:44:23 The executive asks for an update. Pete responds that the group is still looking at what caused it. "We are looking at action items to perform next," he says.

05:49:45 There is further general discussion on the path forward, but with no consensus. After several minutes, the executive says, "Let's move forward."

06:10:43 Discussion on how long the script will run and the need to monitor the time.

06:24:06 One of the SMEs asks about the email issues one customer has, and another SME says she knows nothing about that and she needs more information. An SME provides some background info on the email issue. The SME says, "Let's work on the email issue." There is some discussion, but Pete is silent in this discussion.

06:29:41 Pete reports that the analytics look good and are all green.

06:31:05 Customer Service reports they have checked with a customer and they are able to log in. They are checking with more customers.

06:37:25 Paul asks who is running this bridge, Pete or another SME? Pete offers that he is the leader.

07:02:26 SME reports the new email is coming in, but the old email in the queue is backed up. SME asks for some help in flushing the queue. Pete asks another SME to take care of it. The executive wants to make sure everything is documented for the Root Cause Analysis.

07:13:12 Customer Service says another customer is reporting they are able to log in and do not appear to have any functionality issues. Acme Chemical Sales is only reporting one issue now. SMEs are still investigating. Problem in the chat window.

07:17:00 Pete says, "Looks like email is working again." No objections from the group and the callers begin to drop off the bridge.

07:47:14 There is discussion on root cause between Paul and Pete.

07:50:00 Call is terminated.

CASE STUDY AAR

This incident started as part of a software release (planned work) but turned into an incident. If there are no plans in place to transition from planned work that went poorly and becomes an incident, there should be. An incident action plan (IAP) should be developed for planned work, which outlines the rules of engagement (ROE) if an incident were to occur during the software release. Once it was determined that this planned work was an incident and creating customer impact, a formal incident should have been declared and IMS implemented.

There was a significant amount of time lost during this incident conference call bridge. The team had several options, but they continually rehashed the options. At times, it wasn't clear who was actually still on the incident conference call bridge. The group was essentially leaderless, except for Pete occasionally asking questions.

At no point did anyone declare themselves the Incident Commander. When new SMEs joined the bridge, no one identified themselves as the Incident Commander, nor were any CAN reports provided. Without an Incident Commander, there were no other assigned roles and people were performing actions without direction. Scripts were being run and actions taken without anyone knowing what the SMEs were specifically doing. No one was tracking the activities of the SMEs, nor was anyone making any specific assignments. In short, there was no accountability.

This incident would have benefitted from periodic operational briefings by the Incident Commander in a CAN report format on a regular cadence. In this incident, every 30 minutes would have been best. These briefings would include a review of the options available and quick fact-based decision-making by the Incident Commander. The Incident Commander should instill a sense of urgency to restore service and focus on incident resolution. None of these areas that we like to see were used in this bridge, which contributed to a significant delay. Once it was decided to take action, service was restored in short order.

Once the AAR is completed, an evaluation including a timeline for implementing recommendations as well as a feedback loop for ensuring the recommendations are acted upon should be generated. This is the part where blame is omitted in favor of a purely objective, honest viewpoint on the relationship between the problem, the people, and the solution. Perhaps it is found that the SMEs couldn't identify the problem quickly and there was delay in bringing in more help. Or maybe there were too many people on an incident conference call bridge, and the Incident Commander didn't moderate the discussions. There are a multitude of reasons why an incident response might not go well.

The AAR will certainly point out items that can be addressed immediately, along with items that may be assigned long-term time frames for correction. You can determine the time frames based on schedules and staffing, but it's important to assign the recommended change to a specific person or team and ensure it gets done. Figure 6-3 is a very brief example of documenting the recommendations discovered during the AAR.

Example AAR Recommendations Chart

Action/Activity	Timeline	Assigned Org	Notes
Incorrect phone number for Acme Router company in contact list	Immediate	Site Reliability	Change made by Site Reliability after the incident.
Acme version 3.1.2 being used on Node 6	30 Days - next update/revision cycle on 1/3/18	Network	Other nodes were updated on 12/3/16
Zero Services using new query software - training required	2 months	Site Reliability, Database, Network, and Systems	Training on software to be completed by listed orgs during their refresher training cycle

Figure 6-3. Example recommendation/accountability chart

Some companies choose to record the audio from incident conference call bridges, which is a good way to capture the problem-solving discussion. The audio, however, may capture what is said on a bridge but does not include all other methods of communication used. If there are private conversations, online chats, texts, or other messaging done off the incident conference call bridge, then it may not be captured. One way to include these offline discussions is to announce them on the bridge. As an example, the Incident Commander may have an SMS text message exchange with an SME offline, come back to the bridge, and say, "I had a conversation with SAN/Storage and they have recommended two potential courses of action." The Incident Commander can then give a basic description of the discussion with SAN/Storage. Then everyone on the incident conference call bridge is aware, and it is captured for later review. This is where an Incident Commander acts as a conduit for the entire response and keeps everyone in the loop on the information exchange. Companies have so many varied methods to communicate, which can be both a benefit and a hindrance. Just like the span of control for people, the Incident Commander can only keep track of a limited number of communications channels. It is certainly acceptable to have offline conversations, but a summary of those conversations should be documented for later review.

Note

One important note on documentation: efforts should be made to not only record decisions (either verbal or written), but should also include information on why the decision was made, and what information was available to the IRT when the Incident Commander made the decision. The recording of this information is not to be used for criticism or reprisal. It should be there to document the background/rationale as to why a decision was made, at the time it was made, with the information available.

When the AAR does not have the background as to why a decision was made or who participated in making it, there may be a wrong conclusion reached about why it was made in the first place. Certainly, this can be difficult to document and somewhat subjective, but the basis and discussion points should be documented.

When all the information is compiled and the timeline created, the evaluation of the incident response begins. This is the part where many how/what/why questions get asked—the exploratory/explanatory phase of the response. The key incident responders should convene, look over the information gathered from the five questions listed earlier, and begin to add the commentary. Here are examples of some key questions to dig deeper into during the AAR:

- What were the reasons behind the decisions made?

- What were the challenges encountered during the incident response? Did we have the right tools, people, and other resources?

- What were the communications challenges? (Were incident responders able to get access to information and communicate?)

- What was the behavior of those participating on the incident conference call bridge?

- How quickly did it take to size up the problem and understand what was happening?

Don't forget to acknowledge the good parts, too. Great work and lessons learned should be recognized, reinforced, and praised!

In short, the human factors of the AAR look at the use of the framework (IMS), the focused leadership of Incident Commander (IC), and the process and results of the problem-solving effort (PS). Consider these elements as we return to the incident response equation used in Chapter 1, and look at it revised for the AAR process, as shown in Figure 6-4. These should be measured against the all-important time question—were all incident response dimensions completed in such a way that the incident responders arrived at the best decision in the shortest amount of time? When evaluated like this, conclusions about the effectiveness of the entire incident response as it relates to protecting the business can be drawn.

$$\text{Efficient Incident Response} = \frac{(\text{IMS} + \text{IC}) + \text{PS}}{\text{Time}}$$

Figure 6-4. Incident response equation

Keep in mind that an AAR doesn't have to be complex, and it is up to you how you format the report that results from the AAR process. As Figure 6-3 shows, the main thing is to look at the right elements, which is done by evaluating the functions of response more than the individuals, which also helps to avoid the blame game.

An evaluation of the incident response framework (IMS)	➡	*Who responded to the incident and what did each person contribute?*
An evaluation of the incident responders including the Incident Commander	➡	*How did the IRT perform?*
Description of the business impact	➡	*What was the true cost of the incident as measured by damage to trust, reputation, financial impact, and investor confidence?*

This may demonstrate to the entire organization that technology failures can be costly, and resolving them quickly and efficiently is of paramount importance to protect the value of the business.

Figures Figure 6-5 and Figure 6-6 make up a standardized checklist format to capture the actions taken at the incident generally, as well as the leadership and problem-solving actions. The form is not exhaustive in that it may not depict all the dimensions you might choose to look at. It serves as more of a template for you to build a customized way to memorialize the incident.

How your organization chooses to make the necessary changes, corrective actions, repairs, and other related revisions is beyond the scope of this text, but suffice it say that failing to act on the identified deficiencies makes the entire AAR process significantly less useful. Many organizations don't follow through on recommendations and that leads to lack of confidence in the IRT that the company is serious about making changes to improve operations. Don't expect to get better at responding to incidents if you don't learn from the good and bad things that happened and make the necessary changes!

When it comes to the nontechnology side of evaluating an incident response (soft skills), there is an acronym available to help you to identify or narrow down issues that occur with people and correlate it with a solution. The acronym is *TALENT—training, accountability, leadership, empowerment,* and *notification*—and it's a pretty useful tool.

Blackrock 3 Partners Inc.

GEO: _____ IC: _____ Date: _____ Incident Identifier _____
SEV level _____ Discovery time _____ Resolution time _____

IMS/Incident Commander Review Sheet

The goal of the review is to provide the IC and IMS participants with positive, constructive feedback on the elements listed below. A key outcome of this process will be the improvement of individual skills and group capabilities in managing incidents. It provides a set of criteria upon which to form an opinion on the effectiveness of the response, capture relevant data for notifications and executive briefings, and provide a basis for the AAR.

List incident participants and specialty here:

List incident objective(s) here:

IC identified and announced?
Command transferred? (List reason for transfer)

#	Task Steps	Weight			Awarded
	N = didn't complete, Y = completed P = partially or completed later	N	Y	P	
1.	Size up complete, accurate and articulated?	0	10	5	
2.	Were appropriate SME's requested. SME response times acceptable? If not, list reason why.	0	10	5	
3.	SEV level identified and announced	0	5	2	
4.	Does the IC control the flow of the discussion and drive the incident toward resolution in an effective and timely manner?	0	35	17	
5.	Did the IC adhere to acceptable span of control numbers? (If exceeded was the acceptable? Did the IC control the extra numbers effectively?	0	5	2	
6.	Did the IC establish effective communications?	0	10	5	
7.	Is there an incident timeline and estimated time to resolution?	0	5	2	
8.	Were briefings, notifications and postings made at the appropriate time(s)?	0	10	5	
9.	Did the IC develop a backup plan and/or consider second tier alternatives? Did they assign a plans group to develop a backup plan or forecast?	0	10	5	
10.	Did the IC discuss notifying DR at 30 minutes? Did they make appropriate notifications at the 1-hour mark for potential DR?				
	Total	100%			

Figure 6-5. Page 1 of the standardized checklist format to capture the actions taken at the incident generally, as well as the leadership and problem-solving actions

Blackrock 3 Partners Inc.

Reviewer Comments:

Timeline:

Evaluator: _________Hawley __________ Date: ___5/24/17_______ Time: _______1616 hrs________

Blackrock 3 Partners Inc. – Sensitive and Proprietary Information

Figure 6-6. Page 2 of the standardized checklist format to capture the actions taken at the incident

TRAINING

A lack of appropriate training is a common reason that human errors are made during incident response. It's common for an AAR to identify a training issue relative to the piece of the incident response that wasn't excellent. If poor performance is identified, some prescriptive training is usually indicated. Beware, however, that handling a unique problem where no solution is apparent (red- or black-box incident) does not automatically open the training conversation. Allowances must be made for the complex issues that complex systems create. A training issue might be raised because the Incident Commander allowed the span of control to get too big, or maybe SMEs not trained in IMS practices participated and ultimately disrupted the incident conference call bridge. The complexity or time it takes to solve problems may not indicate training deficiencies.

ACCOUNTABILITY

In some cases, errors or omissions are made because the people making them are not accountable to anyone specific during an incident, when the switch from peacetime to wartime is made. In incident response, roles and responsibilities must be clear. Each person participating in the incident response should be responsible for being operationally ready for wartime; this means they are available, prepared, and ready to respond and contribute. The organization should set company-wide incident response standards so responders understand their time obligation to acknowledge dispatch and respond to the incident conference call bridge with urgency, not just to meet their service level agreements (SLA).

LEADERSHIP

Good incident management depends on solid and firm leadership. Weak Incident Commanders can let an incident slip from their control and the response can quickly get chaotic and disorganized. When no strong direction is offered to the IRT and/or the response objectives and timelines are not clearly identified, unnecessary and preventable downtime occurs. Along with training, it is common for issues of all levels of leadership to be identified as corrective items in an AAR. This is not just pertinent to the Incident Commander. It is also important to determine, especially on high severity events, or when UC is activated, if the executives of the company performed well according to their function on the incident.

EMPOWERMENT

In the world of incident response outside public safety, there may be challenges with responders making decisions that they should be empowered to make. Incidents move fast and the response must move as fast or faster in order to keep up. This requires incident responders to be empowered to make decisions at their level and to take ownership of their piece of the response. If an incident response gets bogged down because the Incident Commander is a micromanager or incident responders are not authorized to take action within their scope, the response will be slow to develop and time will be lost. Those arriving on the incident conference bridge should be the right people with the skills, knowledge, and abilities to act as well as the authority to do so.

NOTIFICATION

In many cases, not having the right people working the problem results in slow resolution. If a company has SLAs in place for incident responders, they should be enforced. Notification(s) to customers, affected business units, or key executives should be outlined during peacetime, prior to the switch to wartime. During an incident response, information becomes a hot commodity. Given the complexity of today's technology stack and sophistication of monitoring tools, it's possible that large amounts of alerts can be generated and lead to "alert fatigue" for the IRT. It is important to make a distinction between events and incidents.

Clearly, monitoring levels must be appropriate to fulfill the business needs of each organization. However, these needs must be balanced to minimize downtime and prevent burnout of the IRT. Part of establishing a culture of incident response in an organization is this reality: *incidents should be treated as something until proven that they are nothing, rather than nothing until it's discovered that they are something.* If the latter is the culture of the organization, valuable time will be lost on every incident response, which will have a detrimental effect on the business. Using this methodology will elongate MMTA and it's where many organizations lose valuable time.

TRUST

Trust is a tougher dimension to pin down in any one way, but it is worth considering as a broader point to ponder during an AAR. As an example, if the real reason an event went sideways was because the incident responders didn't trust each other to do their respective job, or if senior management bypassed the Incident Commander and unofficially wrestled control from the formal Incident Commander, those are issues of trust that should be addressed in the AAR. Most of the impediments in improving your MTTR metric will be in the culture of the organization, and culture is purely driven by people.

To sum up TALENT, think of it as a filter for identifying performance or process gaps. All you have to do is identify the problem, run it through the elements of TALENT, and the place upon which you should focus the remediation is usually pretty apparent.

AAR Case Study: The New SME

Let's look at a fictional situation that occurred during an incident, and how TALENT can be used to quickly isolate a people problem. This situation was logged in an entry of the incident documentation and brought up during the AAR.

> The Incident Commander tasked an SME with contacting a vendor. The SME was a new DBA to the company and had no previous experience in incident response. The SME's experience and expertise was solely in DBA development work, not responding to incidents. The SME had no idea how to contact the vendor, left the incident conference call bridge without checking in with the Incident Commander, and started calling colleagues to get the answer. Unfortunately, it was late on a weekend night and the SME couldn't get in touch with anyone quickly. While the SME was searching for the contact information for the vendor, the Incident Commander recognized the DBA function had dropped from the incident conference call bridge and called for another DBA.
>
> After the new DBA arrived, the Incident Commander assigned the new DBA the task of contacting the vendor. The original DBA located the vendor's contact information and asked the vendor to join the incident conference call bridge. As the vendor joined the incident conference call bridge, both the Incident Commander and the second DBA were confused and asked questions of the vendor. The first DBA responded by saying the assignment of getting the vendor was complete, but the second DBA was still trying to contact the same vendor. The vendor quickly identified the problem and it was resolved in 15 minutes. The result? The company had a customer with 1,000 users that could not access their website for almost 45 minutes. Is the SME at fault for poor performance? Could the incident have been resolved in a shorter amount of time?

Let's break the SME issue into individual elements, with some additional facts that were learned during the AAR.

ISSUE IDENTIFIED DURING THE AAR

The SME was designated as the primary DBA SME without knowledge of the SME's role in IMS or how to contact one of the company's vendors. The senior DBA that was originally supposed to be on-call decided at the last minute to take vacation and the manager appointed the new DBA as the on-call because no other DBA wanted to work over the weekend. The company does have a training program for IRT members, but the first DBA hadn't been trained as to the rules of engagement for SMEs in IMS or the expectations of the Incident Commander.

From the first DBA's perspective, their actions were appropriate. From the Incident Commander's perspective, the first DBA's actions were not appropriate. From the second DBA's perspective, there was confusion. From the vendor's perspective, the IRT looked unorganized. There was duplication of effort and no accountability. Getting the vendor on the incident conference call bridge was delayed, causing unnecessary downtime. Most importantly, from the customer's perspective, they experienced downtime when they pay for uptime!

CHANGE RECOMMENDATIONS FROM THE AAR

Ensure that any incident responder tasked with response should be fully trained prior to taking on the responsibilities. It seems simple, but it's very possible to jump to the conclusion that a good engineer should be a good incident responder. All you need are good technical skills to be on the IRT, right? Not true! Incident response is a process unto itself and requires skills, knowledge, and abilities unique to participating in the IMS process, separate and apart from the technical skills of engineering.

The big question is why this occurred and how it should be addressed. To keep the corrective action honed in on the reason, just run the problem statement through the TALENT acronym and the answer will generally be pretty evident. In this case, the failure of the SME to understand their role in IMS and access the contact list in a timely manner was a simple training issue (the "T" in TALENT). There is leadership (the "L" in TALENT) failure associated with it as well, as the SME supervisor may have dropped the ball in getting the SME up to speed prior to putting them on the IRT to respond.

The corrective action is clear: provide the training to that SME and subsequent SMEs. Perhaps a new procedure is a fix for this in the future. This is a system failure, really, and not the fault of the SME. It would be easy to say the DBA should have known better, and to point the finger at him, but truly the issue is about a PROCESS failure rather than individual performance.

Summary

To conduct an effective AAR, you first must establish a person or team knowledgeable enough to have opinions on the elements you choose to evaluate. A generalist approach is good, but you may have to recruit technical experts to delve into the deeper aspects of technology failures or SME problem-solving efforts. If you suspect that the database was an issue on an incident response, perhaps a DBA-weighted group should be assembled to look at the incident. The main point is to assemble the right group to evaluate the incident.

Some organizations have a defined group that performs all AARs regardless of the nature of the problem. Others put together an AAR team on an ad hoc basis. In either case, the group should always include persons skilled in the framework of IMS, the role of the Incident Commander, and the SME problem-solvers. When assembling the team, personality traits and cooperation among the AAR evaluators are important aspects. A team that you know is going to clash is not going to be effective. You want a group that will openly, and without bias, discuss real issues to provide real and objective observations and recommendations on fixing problems.

The key elements of an AAR are the following:

- Combine relevant documents and communications from the incident.

- Develop an incident timeline.

- Gather relevant participation.

- Foster an open, honest, and blameless forum for the AAR.

- Encourage active discussion among AAR participants.

- Identify solutions or improvements to the people part of the response as well as the technology problems encountered.

- Implement the improvements.

It's quite common for the AAR process to be used to determine who is at fault for a problem. This is completely opposite of the true goal: to improve incident response, determine what broke and how people responded to the thing that broke, and determine what steps need to be taken to prevent a similar situation from happening again.

The AAR can take many forms, and you should develop a format that works for your company. First, look at what caused the problem. Second, evaluate the various parts of the incident response: IMS, Incident Commander, and problem-solving (PS) effort. Third, compile the incident information and write the report as soon as you can. Fourth, convene the IRT to review the findings. Fifth, ensure that changes are identified and, more importantly, followed up on.

Use the TALENT acronym to identify potential areas of improvement or areas where the people part of the incident response performed well or poorly.

Index

About the Authors

Rob Schnepp's emergency response career spans 30 years in international public safety as a Special Operations Fire Chief, Incident Commander, consultant and published author. Rob commanded numerous large-scale emergencies for the Alameda County (CA) Fire Department, protecting 500 square miles and two national laboratories in the East Bay of the San Francisco Bay Area. Rob has responded on Unified Command/Incident Management Teams to high profile incidents including: 9/11 World Trade Center terrorist attack; oil spills in San Francisco Bay (Cosco Busan and Dubai Star); large propane gas explosions; campaign wildland fires and numerous large scale emergencies. Rob planned and directed Red Command at Urban Shield, the largest Homeland Security exercise in the United States. Rob has planned and directed full scale exercises for the Department of Defense in 12 countries.

Rob is on the curriculum development team and teaches Special Operations at the U.S. Fire Administration's National Fire Academy. Rob authored *Hazardous Materials: Awareness and Operations* and serves on the *Fire Engineering* magazine editorial advisory board, and the Fire Department Instructors Conference executive advisory board. Rob is a member of National Fire Protection Association (NFPA) Technical Standards Committee Technical Committee for Hazardous Materials Response Personnel NFPA 472.

Rob has developed risk assessment, incident management and incident command training for Fortune 500 companies, foreign governments, and US national laboratories.

Ron Vidal's corporate career spans 35 years as a senior executive in critical infrastructure including fiber optic networks (metro/long haul/subsea), data centers, oil & gas, power systems and capital markets. Previously, Ron was a senior executive at Level 3 Communication (operated 16,000 mile international metro, long haul and transoceanic fiber optic Tier 1 backbone network), UUNet Technologies (largest Tier 1 Internet Service Provider (ISP) when acquired by MFS), MFS Communications (operated 38 metro fiber networks in U.S. and Europe, acquired by Worldcom) and Kiewit Construction (3rd largest U.S. construction contractor).

Ron led technical and operational due diligence teams on over $19 billion of telecommunications and Internet Mergers & Acquisitions (M&A) transactions, including the 5th largest transaction in history at its closing. Ron developed and communicated key financial messages during the sale of $14 billion of public equity, debt and convertible debt securities, across 10 international roadshows and 8 trading desks, and managed relationships with 21 sell-side research analysts and 25 of Level 3's largest shareholders and bondholders. Ron presented at investment conferences sponsored by Goldman Sachs, Citigroup, Morgan Stanley, Merrill Lynch, Bank of America, Credit Suisse, UBS, Oppenheimer and others and at company sponsored investor & analyst days and has been quoted in *Business Week, USA TodayItalicized Text* and numerous trade publications.

Ron led Level 3 Communications relief and recovery efforts in New York City after the 9/11 World Trade Center terrorist attack. Ron also served on Mayor Dinkins New York City Task Force on Network Reliability and currently serves on the California Cybersecurity Task Force. Ron has advocated technology public policy to Members and staff of United States Congress, Commissioners and staff of the Federal Communications Commission (FCC) and Commissioners and staff of the California, Illinois, Massachusetts and New York Public Utility Commissions (PUC), notably testifying before the House Subcommittee on Telecommunications and the Internet on E-911 and Voice over Internet Protocol (VoIP) policy. Ron is a volunteer firefighter, and former Chair of the Emergency Preparedness Commission in Mill Valley, California and a technical peer reviewer for FEMA's Assistance for Firefighter Grant (AFG) program. In total, Ron has served on twelve federal, state and local task forces, commissions and grant making panels and seven non-profit Boards.

Chris Hawley's emergency response career spans 30 years. Most recently, Chris's team managed a Department of Defense (DoD) program that provides training and exercises for countering the threat spectrum of chemical, biological, radiological, nuclear and high yield explosive (CBRNE) threats globally. The team conducted in-country assessments with Ministry level and U.S. Embassy personnel in major cities and ports of entry, develops a plan to deliver training and equipment to the host nation and designs and conducts progressive and escalating exercises for single nation Ministries to multiple nation, multiple day Weapons of Mass Destruction (WMD) events. Chris has conducted training and exercises in 40 countries.

Chris codeveloped the FBI's Hazardous Materials Operations training program, Hazardous Materials Technician Program and SWAT Tactical Operations training program, serving as course manager and instructor for many of their specialized assets. He also co-developed the Department of Justice Crime Scene Management program, and WMD Evidence Management course.

Chris also served as Deputy Administrator for the Emergency Management Division and Special Operations Coordinator for Hazardous Materials Response and Advanced Technical Rescue for Baltimore County (MD) Fire Department, the 5th largest U.S. fire department, that protects 610 square miles including the Port of Baltimore and Interstate 95.

Since 1995, Chris has served as the Conference Planning Chair for the International Hazardous Materials Response Teams Conference, which is the largest worldwide conference of its type and is sponsored by the International Association of Fire Chiefs (IAFC). Chris is a technical working group member of the National Fire Protection Association (NFPA) Hazardous Materials 472 standards committee, which is used worldwide and outlines the training requirements for hazardous materials and WMD response.

Chris has authored the following textbooks: *Hazardous Materials Incidents* (3rd Edition); *Hazardous Materials Air Monitoring & Detection Devices* (2nd Edition); *Hazardous Materials Response & Operations*; and co-authored *Special Operations: For Terrorism and Hazmat Crimes*. These texts have been adopted in WMD programs in the FBI, Secret Service, Department of Defense Emergency Response Training program and the Federal Law Enforcement Training Center. A number of states use these textbooks as part of their mandatory training programs for all emergency responders. In addition to writing numerous articles in trade magazines, Chris is also an Editorial Board member for *HazMat Responder World Magazine*. Chris is a member of National Fire Protection Association (NFPA) Technical Standards Committee Technical Committee for Hazardous Materials Response Personnel NFPA 472.

Chris serves as a technical consultant to numerous manufacturers for product, services and new technology development in the fields of air monitoring, hazardous materials and terrorism response. Chris conducts threat assessments and on-site building vulnerability assessments for protection against terrorism threats and attacks. In addition to those listed above, Chris has developed, or participated and delivered training programs for US Marines Chemical & Biological Response Force, National Security Agency, U.S. Fire Administration's National Fire Academy, and various state and local police agencies. In addition, he has provided training and consultation to more than 50 companies and cities, some of the companies include DuPont, Allied Signal, Honeywell, Northrup Grumman, Smiths Detection, Thermo Scientific, Battelle, SAIC, and a number of military assets. He has provided training for cities in 43 states.

Colophon

The cover fonts are Gotham Condensed Book and Gotham Condensed Medium, the text font is Scala Pro, and the heading font is Benton Sans.

Learn from experts.
Find the answers you need.

Sign up for a **10-day free trial** to get **unlimited access** to all of the content on Safari, including Learning Paths, interactive tutorials, and curated playlists that draw from thousands of ebooks and training videos on a wide range of topics, including data, design, DevOps, management, business—and much more.

Start your free trial at:
oreilly.com/safari

(No credit card required.)

Milton Keynes UK
Ingram Content Group UK Ltd.
UKHW011009150324
439468UK00009B/606